MANHATTAN PREP

Integrated Reasoning & Essay

GMAT Strategy Guide

This guide covers the Integrated Reasoning and Argument Essay sections on the GMAT.
Master the IR question types and discover strategies
for optimizing performance on the essay.

guide **9**

Integrated Reasoning & Essay GMAT Strategy Guide, Sixth Edition

10-digit International Standard Book Number: 1-941234-04-6
13-digit International Standard Book Number: 978-1-941234-04-4
eISBN: 978-1-941234-25-9

Layout Design: Dan McNaney and Cathy Huang
Cover Design: Dan McNaney and Frank Callaghan
Cover Photography: Alli Ugosoli

SUSTAINABLE FORESTRY INITIATIVE
Certified Sourcing
www.sfiprogram.org
SFI-00756

GMAT® STRATEGY GUIDES

0	GMAT Roadmap	**5**	Number Properties
1	Fractions, Decimals, & Percents	**6**	Critical Reasoning
2	Algebra	**7**	Reading Comprehension
3	Word Problems	**8**	Sentence Correction
4	Geometry	**9**	Integrated Reasoning & Essay

STRATEGY GUIDE SUPPLEMENTS

Math

GMAT Foundations of Math

GMAT Advanced Quant

Verbal

GMAT Foundations of Verbal

MANHATTAN
PREP

December 2nd, 2014

Dear Student,

Thank you for picking up a copy of *Integrated Reasoning & Essay*. I hope this book gives you just the guidance you need to get the most out of your GMAT studies.

A great number of people were involved in the creation of the book you are holding. First and foremost is Zeke Vanderhoek, the founder of Manhattan Prep. Zeke was a lone tutor in New York City when he started the company in 2000. Now, well over a decade later, the company contributes to the successes of thousands of students around the globe every year.

Our Manhattan Prep Strategy Guides are based on the continuing experiences of our instructors and students. The overall vision of the 6th Edition GMAT guides was developed by Stacey Koprince, Whitney Garner, and Dave Mahler over the course of many months; Stacey and Whitney then led the execution of that vision as the primary author and editor, respectively, of this book. Numerous other instructors made contributions large and small, but I'd like to send particular thanks to Josh Braslow, Kim Cabot, Dmitry Farber, Ron Purewal, Emily Meredith Sledge, and Ryan Starr. Dan McNaney and Cathy Huang provided design and layout expertise as Dan managed book production, while Liz Krisher made sure that all the moving pieces, both inside and outside of our company, came together at just the right time. Finally, we are indebted to all of the Manhattan Prep students who have given us feedback over the years. This book wouldn't be half of what it is without your voice.

At Manhattan Prep, we aspire to provide the best instructors and resources possible, and we hope that you will find our commitment manifest in this book. We strive to keep our books free of errors, but if you think we've goofed, please post to manhattanprep.com/GMAT/errata. If you have any questions or comments in general, please email our Student Services team at gmat@manhattanprep.com. Or give us a shout at 212-721-7400 (or 800-576-4628 in the U.S. or Canada). I look forward to hearing from you.

Thanks again, and best of luck preparing for the GMAT!

Sincerely,

Chris Ryan
Vice President of Academics
Manhattan Prep

HOW TO ACCESS YOUR ONLINE RESOURCES

IF YOU ARE A REGISTERED MANHATTAN PREP STUDENT

and have received this book as part of your course materials, you have AUTOMATIC access to ALL of our online resources. This includes all practice exams, question banks, and online updates to this book. To access these resources, follow the instructions in the Welcome Guide provided to you at the start of your program. Do NOT follow the instructions below.

IF YOU PURCHASED THIS BOOK FROM MANHATTANPREP.COM OR AT ONE OF OUR CENTERS

1. Go to: **www.manhattanprep.com/gmat/studentcenter**
2. Log in with the username and password you chose when setting up your account.

IF YOU PURCHASED THIS BOOK AT A RETAIL LOCATION

1. Go to: **www.manhattanprep.com/gmat/access**
2. Create an account or, if you already have one, log in on this page with your username and password.
3. Follow the instructions on the screen.

Your one year of online access begins on the day that you register your book at the above URL.

You only need to register your product ONCE at the above URL. To use your online resources any time AFTER you have completed the registration process, log in to the following URL:

www.manhattanprep.com/gmat/studentcenter

Please note that online access is nontransferable. This means that only NEW and UNREGISTERED copies of the book will grant you online access. Previously used books will NOT provide any online resources.

IF YOU PURCHASED AN EBOOK VERSION OF THIS BOOK

1. Create an account with Manhattan Prep at this website:

www.manhattanprep.com/gmat/register

2. Email a copy of your purchase receipt to **gmat@manhattanprep.com** to activate your resources. Please be sure to use the same email address to create an account that you used to purchase the eBook.

For any questions, email **gmat@manhattanprep.com** or call **800-576-4628**.

Please refer to the following page for a description of the online resources that come with this book.

YOUR ONLINE RESOURCES

YOUR PURCHASE INCLUDES ONLINE ACCESS TO THE FOLLOWING:

1 FULL-LENGTH GMAT PRACTICE EXAM

The full-length GMAT practice exam included with this book is delivered online using Manhattan Prep's proprietary computer-adaptive test engine. The exam adapts to your ability level by drawing from a bank of more than 500 unique questions of varying difficulty levels written by Manhattan Prep's expert instructors, all of whom have scored in the 99th percentile on the Official GMAT. At the end of the exam you will receive a score, an analysis of your results, and the opportunity to review detailed explanations for each question.

Important Note: The GMAT exam included with the purchase of this book is the same exam that you receive upon purchasing any book in the Manhattan Prep GMAT Complete Strategy Guide Set.

5 FREE INTERACT™ LESSONS

Interact™ is a comprehensive self-study program that is fun, intuitive, and directed by you. Each interactive video lesson is taught by an expert Manhattan Prep instructor and includes dozens of individual branching points. The choices you make determine the content you see. This book comes with access to the first five lessons of GMAT Interact. Lessons are available on your computer or iPad so you can prep where you are, when you want. For more information on the full version of this program, visit **manhattanprep.com/gmat/interact**.

INTEGRATED REASONING & ESSAY ONLINE QUESTION BANK

The Online Question Bank for Integrated Reasoning & Essay consists of 25 extra practice questions (with detailed explanations) that test the variety of concepts and skills covered in this book. These questions provide you with extra practice beyond the problem sets contained in this book. You may use our online timer to practice your pacing by setting time limits for each question in the bank.

ONLINE UPDATES TO THE CONTENT IN THIS BOOK

The content presented in this book is updated periodically to ensure that it reflects the GMAT's most current trends. You may view all updates, including any known errors or changes, upon registering for online access.

The above resources can be found in your Student Center at manhattanprep.com/gmat/studentcenter.

TABLE *of* CONTENTS

guide 9

Chapter 1
of
Integrated Reasoning

How to Use This Guide

In This Chapter...

The Essay

Integrated Reasoning

Chapter 1

How to Use This Guide

The *Integrated Reasoning & Essay GMAT Strategy Guide* will help you prepare for the Integrated Reasoning (IR) and Analytical Writing Assessment (AWA, or Argument Essay) sections of the GMAT.

We've put together this chapter to help you get the most out of this guide and any other resources you use as you prepare for these two sections.

The Essay

The Argument Essay is the first section of the test as well as the least important. For most people, it's sufficient to earn a score of 4 or higher (out of 6).

Because the essay section is first, it's important to make sure that you're prepared to score a 4 or higher while expending the minimum necessary mental energy.

As a result, you have two main goals for your essay preparation:

1. Put yourself in a position to score 4 or higher.
2. Have a mental template in place to make it as easy as possible to write the essay.

For many, working through the essay chapter of this book will be enough to accomplish those two goals. If you have access to our GMAT Interact™ for Essay lesson, you can use this resource in addition to or instead of the essay chapter in this book.

If you are struggling to compose complex sentences, Appendix A of this book will teach you how to write better sentences. This appendix is especially useful for anyone who doesn't have much practice writing complex prose in English.

Test your skills on GMAC's GMAT Write™ program, the same software scoring system used on the real exam. For a small fee, you'll get a score and feedback on two essays. You'll be able to revise the essays and submit them again to see whether your score improves. If you're already in one of our programs, check your program details; you might already have access to GMAT Write for free.

1

Integrated Reasoning

IR is the second section of the test. Most people will want to score a minimum of 5 or 6 (out of 8) on this section.

The IR section also falls before the main event, Quant and Verbal, so you will again want to make sure you're in a position to get a good enough score while not expending too much mental energy.

Start with Chapter 3, "Introduction to Integrated Reasoning," to familiarize yourself with the timing, scoring, and structure of this section, including the four types of IR problems.

Chapters 4–7 cover the four problem types, one per chapter. We've organized the chapters into what we think is the best order in which to study the four types, but if you want to jump around, you can. Later chapters do not build on or rely on the earlier ones.

Chapter 8 summarizes the strategies for each problem type and for the overall IR section. Appendix B summarizes some of the decimals, percents, ratios, and statistics topics that are tested on the IR section. For full treatment of these topics, see our *Fractions, Decimals, & Percents GMAT Strategy Guide* and our *Word Problems GMAT Strategy Guide*.

Spread your IR study out over the full length of your GMAT preparation. For example, if you're planning to study for 4 months in total, leave the final 2 weeks for a comprehensive review. Your primary studies will therefore be spread over about 3.5 months. At this rate, you should plan to study one IR question type, and complete all associated lessons and exercises, every 2.5–3 weeks.

As you finish a chapter, practice your skills using the online Question Banks that come with this guide. If you purchase the *The Official Guide for GMAT Review* from GMAC® (the makers of the GMAT), you'll have access to an additional online Question Bank of real IR questions from past administrations of the GMAT. GMAC® also offers the IR Prep Tool, an additional online study tool with a number of additional official IR problems.

If you're taking our course, then follow the syllabus that comes with the course. If you have access to our online GMAT Interact for IR lessons, incorporate those into your studies as well. The interactive modules are more detailed, so read the relevant chapter in this book first, then go through the corresponding Interact lesson.

Finally, make sure to include the IR section when taking practice computer-adaptive tests (CATs). You'll gain valuable practice under testing conditions and see whether you're making progress towards your goal score. (If you take your first CAT before you start studying for IR, then you can skip the IR section. After that, though, don't skip IR!)

You're ready to dive into the book. Good luck and happy studying!

Chapter 2

of

Integrated Reasoning

The Argument Essay

In This Chapter...

Chapter 2
The Argument Essay

The GMAT begins with its most open-ended task: the Analytical Writing Assessment (AWA), also known as the Argument Essay, or just the essay. Whether you find this task straightforward or challenging, you will need to familiarize yourself with this piece of the GMAT.

What Is the Argument Essay?

This section of the GMAT consists of one 30-minute essay that you type into the computer. In this essay, you'll examine a flawed argument very similar to the flawed arguments you see on Critical Reasoning (CR) problems.

The essay is separately scored—it does not factor into your general GMAT score (200–800). The scale runs from 0 (lowest) to 6 (highest) in half-point increments. You'll be assessed on three sets of skills:

1. *Logical analysis:* how well do you dissect and evaluate the argument?
2. *Persuasive writing:* how clearly and convincingly do you express your thoughts?
3. *Language usage:* grammar, syntax, variety of vocabulary

Chapter 11, "Analytical Writing Assessment," of *The Official Guide for GMAT Review* describes the essay task and provides a few useful example essays, as well as a list of possible essay topics and other useful material. In an appendix, the *Official Gudie* also outlines the AWA scoring scale and corresponding percentiles of a large set of recent test-takers.

2

AWA Score	Label	Percentile
6.0	Outstanding	92
5.5		81
5.0	Strong	60
4.5		44
4.0	Adequate	21
3.5		13
3.0	Limited	6
2.5		5
2.0	Seriously Flawed	3
1.5		3
1.0	Fundamentally Deficient	3
0.5		3
0.0	No Score	0

A 6.0 essay "presents a cogent, well-articulated critique of the argument and demonstrates mastery of the elements of effective writing," though there may still be minor flaws. At the other end of the spectrum, *No score* means you've left the essay blank, written something off topic or in a language other than English (including gibberish), or just recopied the topic.

Performance of Test-Takers

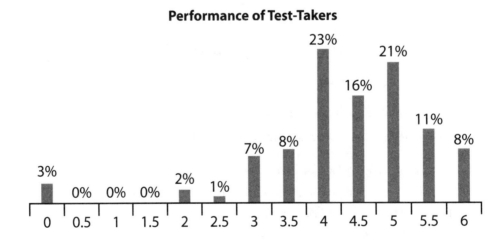

Notice from the above chart that 79% of test-takers score "Adequate" (4.0) or better, while nearly half (40%) score "Strong" (5.0) or better. Both a computer and a human (or two) grade your essay so, unlike your other scores, you won't receive your AWA score until two to three weeks after your test, when you receive your official score report from GMAC®.

MANHATTAN
PREP

What is the purpose of this essay in the admissions process?

It is *not* to distinguish exceptional performance from strong or even adequate performance. An "Outstanding" essay will not improve your admissions chances more than a "Strong" essay will.

In a March 2011 research report, the GMAT folks admit that for the general population of applicants, AWA scores add very little to the power of the GMAT and undergraduate grades to predict academic performance in business school.

So why is this essay on the GMAT? To catch the bottom 20% of scores.

The schools want to ensure that you can write in English well enough to handle graduate-level academic coursework conducted in English, particularly if you are a non-native-English speaker. This essay is the only thing that schools know that you wrote completely on your own. The AWA score provides admissions officers with a "Fine" or "Not Fine" on your ability to write in English.

If you score a 4.5 or higher, the schools will check off the "Fine!" box for you. If, on the other hand, you score a 3.5 or lower, the schools will have concerns. They will likely review the actual text of your essay in order to determine whether they think you can handle business-school-level communications. (Note: if your score is fine, they won't bother to look at the essay text; in that case, they'll just evaluate the essays you hand in as part of your application.)

In short, getting a low score (bottom 20%) on the essay can hurt your chances of admission.

Your goal on the essay is to clear the bar cleanly with a 4.5 or higher.

What about a 4.0? This score is probably fine for admission to any school. After all, a 4.0 is labeled "Adequate." If the rest of your scores are good, don't re-take the test just to lift your AWA score.

That said, if you're going to retake the GMAT anyway, put in a little more time on AWA preparation, so that you clear the hurdle with a little more room. In addition, if you're at all worried about how schools are going to perceive your facility with academic English, then a 4.5 or better can help set your (and their) mind at ease.

If you are relatively confident that you'll score a 4.5 or higher, then you can do minimal preparation:
- Read the rest of this chapter and follow the instructions in "How to Prepare for the Essay."
  - Do GMAT Write™ (you'll learn what this is later in this chapter).
  - Do the essay when taking practice computer-adaptive tests (CATs).
- Go in with a game plan. Know the process you want to follow.
- Write a decent amount. Longer essays generally score higher.
- Treat the essay as a warm-up, saving your energy for the rest of the GMAT.

2

However, if you think you're at risk of a score below a 4.0, then you've got more work to do. To judge your risk, ask yourself these questions:

- *Do you have little experience writing academic English?*
  - Did you rarely write essays in English in school?
  - Were your grades in English classes low?
  - In your job, do you rarely write anything longer or more formal than short emails?
- *Is your command of written academic English weak?*

  If you're unsure, choose a long Reading Comprehension (RC) passage at random and read it with no time pressure, then consider these questions:
  - Are there many words that you didn't understand?
  - Did you fail to understand sentences when they got too long?
  - Did you take 10 minutes or more to finish the passage, only to find that you had little idea what it meant?
  - Did you frequently translate back into another language?
- *Is your command of spoken English weak?*
  - Do you struggle to keep up with a conversation among native English speakers?
  - Do you have a lot more trouble understanding English over the phone than in person?
  - Do you frequently strain to formulate new or complex ideas in English?

If you answered "Yes" to several of these questions, read this chapter carefully and follow up with Appendix A of this guide.

The Physical Mechanics of Essay Writing

You will be typing your essay into a text box on the computer screen. You can enter as much text as you want, but you can only see about 10 lines at once.

The system feels like a clunky, old-fashioned word-processing program. You have just a few buttons with standard functions:

Button	Function	Keyboard Shortcuts
Cut	Cuts text and puts it on a clipboard.	Ctrl-X or Alt-T
Copy	Copies text onto the clipboard.	Ctrl-C or Alt-C
Paste	Pastes text from the clipboard.	Ctrl-V or Alt-P
Undo	Undoes the last edit you made. You can undo your last 10 edits.	Ctrl-Z or Alt-U
Redo	Redoes something you just undid. You can redo the last 10 undone actions.	Ctrl-Y or Alt-R

Navigation keys on the keyboard act as you expect:

Arrow Keys move the cursor up, down, left, or right.

Enter and *Return* insert a paragraph bre ak and move you to a new line.

Page Up moves the cursor up one screen.

Page Down moves the cursor down one screen.

Backspace removes the character to the left of the cursor.

Delete removes the character to the right of the cursor.

Home moves the cursor to the beginning of the line.

End moves the cursor to the end of the line.

There is no underline, *italic*, or **bold**. Do not use any text-message substitutes (e.g., *asterisks* or ALL CAPS). Rely on the words themselves to convey emphasis.

There is no tab or indent. To start a new paragraph, hit Return a couple of times to insert a blank line between paragraphs. If you like to indent the beginning of paragraphs, hit the space bar a small, consistent number of times (say, five).

There is no spell check or grammar check. Good spelling and grammar are better than bad spelling and grammar, of course, so do your best in the moment to avoid mistakes, but don't labor excessively. Follow spelling and grammatical rules well enough to make your meaning clear, but keep writing.

What the Argument Essay Asks

The Argument Essay asks you to analyze an argument—something with a conclusion and premises, as you've learned on Critical Reasoning. In fact, your CR tools will come in handy as you tackle the essay.

The argument that you need to analyze will contain a conclusion, or big claim, along with a few premises. Here's an invented, slightly extreme example:

> The country of Tarquinia has a much higher rate of traffic accidents per person than its neighbors, and in the vast majority of cases one or more drivers is found to be at fault in the courts. Therefore, Tarquinia should abolish driver-side seatbelts, airbags, and other safety measures that protect the driver, while new cars should be installed with a spike on the steering column pointed at the driver's heart. These measures will eliminate traffic accidents in Tarquinia by motivating drivers to drive safely.

Here, the conclusion is that *these measures* (abolishing driver-side safety measures and installing the death spike) *will eliminate traffic accidents in Tarquinia by motivating drivers to drive safely*. The premises are listed in the first sentence: the high rate of traffic accidents and the finding of driver fault. The second sentence describes the proposed measures and can be seen as part of the conclusion.

These are the official instructions for the essay:

> Discuss how well reasoned you find this argument. In your discussion, be sure to analyze the line of reasoning and the use of evidence in the argument. For example, you may need to consider what questionable assumptions underlie the thinking and what alternative explanations or counterexamples might weaken the conclusion. You can also discuss what sort of evidence would strengthen or refute the argument, what changes in the argument would make it more logically sound, and what, if anything, would help you better evaluate its conclusion.

Let's break these four sentences down. The first sentence is the most important:

Sentence 1: *Discuss how well reasoned you find this argument.*

The argument will *never* be very well reasoned! Your goal is to find the flaws and explain them clearly.

Sentence 2: *In your discussion, be sure to analyze the line of reasoning and the use of evidence in the argument.*

Line of reasoning
- Does the conclusion follow completely logically from the premises? (No!) Why not?
- What and where are the gaps? Under what circumstances does the logic fail?
- What would help the author prove the conclusion?

Use of evidence
- Does the evidence truly prove what the author wants it to? (No!) Why not?
- What does the given evidence actually prove? Under what circumstances?

Sentence 3: *For example, you may need to consider what questionable assumptions underlie the thinking and what alternative explanations or counterexamples might weaken the conclusion.*

Questionable assumptions
- At each stage of the logic, what has the author assumed that is not necessarily justified?

Alternative explanations or counterexamples
- What else might explain the facts?
- What situations, cases, or circumstances has the author overlooked?

Sentence 4: *You can also discuss what sort of evidence would strengthen or refute the argument, what changes in the argument would make it more logically sound, and what, if anything, would help you better evaluate its conclusion.*

The last items listed in the instructions are worthwhile but *less* important. You can get a 6.0 without including any of these aspects.

You are not asked to argue *for* or *against* the conclusion. Don't say whether you agree or disagree with it. Rather, pretend a friend has asked you to vet his argument before he presents it to his boss. Help him analyze the logical strength of his argument: how well the conclusion is supported by the premises.

How to Manage Your Time

To write a decent essay in only 30 minutes, you'll need a clear process, such as the five-step one below:

1. Read (1–2 min)
2. Brainstorm (2 min)
3. Outline (1–2 min)
4. Write (20 min)
5. Polish—a little (3–5 min)

Here's a short description of each step. You'll learn more about steps 2, 3, and 4 later in this chapter.

Step 1: Read (1–2 min)

First, clear your mind and read the argument slowly and carefully. Don't race through the reading. Thirty minutes is not very long, but if you don't take time to understand the argument, you won't write a very good essay.

As you read, identify the conclusion—the big claim that the author is making. The rest of the argument typically consists of background information and premises—facts and smaller claims made to support the conclusion. This support will always be flawed in some way and those flaws will be based on gaps between the premises and the conclusion. Your job is to find those gaps.

Step 2: Brainstorm (2 min)

Some flaws will jump right out at you; others may take some thought. Jot your ideas on the scrap paper or type them directly into the computer. Either way, don't write too much at this point—just enough to remind you of your thoughts.

Step 3: Outline (1–2 min)

Type a short placeholder into the text box for each paragraph, including an introduction, some body paragraphs, and a conclusion.

Step 4. Write (20 min)

Now go to town. The three scored examples in the *Official Guide* show a clear pattern:

Score	Word Count
6.0	335
4.0	260
2.0	108

The example of a 6.0 on mba.com (an essay that was actually written by a test-taker) has 599 words! There's no need to write that much, but do write a decent amount. Aim for around 300 words.

Conveying complex information typically requires complex sentences. In fact, higher-scoring students typically write longer sentences than lower-scoring ones:

Score	Word Count	Sentences	Words per Sentence
6.0	335	13	25.8
6.0 (mba.com)	599	26	23.0
4.0	260	15	17.3
2.0	108	8	13.5

Train yourself to write approximately 20 words a sentence, not as a strict measure to apply in every case, but rather as a rough average. If you write 15 sentences averaging 20 words per sentence, you'll have 300 words (though one very short sentence can really stand out when you have an important point to make). Later in this chapter, you'll learn more about how to write better GMAT sentences.

Step 5. Polish—a Little (3–5 min)

With a few minutes to go, turn off the spigot. Glance back over what you've written and smooth out the worst of the rough edges. Don't take too much time on any one sentence, gnawing your pen to find the *mot juste* (the "perfect word" in French); you only need a *good enough* score on the essay. Don't try to be Shakespeare.

In fact, if you're confident about the essay, you might want to finish a minute or so early. You don't get a break before Integrated Reasoning, but you can make your own mini-break by finishing your essay slightly early and then waiting to hit Submit. Don't worry—if you somehow don't actually hit the button, what you've written will still be submitted.

During your self-made break, you won't be able to get up and walk around, but you are able to close your eyes, take a few deep breaths, roll your shoulders, and massage your neck. The extra seconds you take to manage your bodily state will do you good going into IR, which you will probably find more challenging.

How to Generate Good Ideas

As mentioned earlier, you'll need to brainstorm several flaws from the argument.

The key to brainstorming is to follow a method, four of which are described below. Try them out and use the method that works best for you.

Whichever method you use, jot down just enough to capture the idea; you don't have much time. Then look for another idea. Here's how: imagine that the flaw that you just spotted is now fixed. What *else* is wrong with the argument? Once you've identified three (or more) flaws, move to the outline phase.

Brainstorming Method 1: Line by Line

Start with the first sentence in the argument. What's wrong with it?

- If it's a piece of evidence, how does it fall short in proving the bigger point?

- If it's a claim, how is it not supported by the evidence?

Work your way, sentence by sentence, to the end of the argument.

Brainstorming Method 2: The CAST System

CAST is an acronym to remind you what you're looking for:

Counterexamples
- What situations would disprove the author's assertions?

Assumptions
- What is the author assuming, probably in an unjustified way?

Strengthen
- What would strengthen the argument?

Terms
- What specific words in the argument create logical gaps or other problems?

Go letter by letter through CAST and jot down ideas.

Brainstorming Method 3: Use the Instructions

You'll always be provided with the same instructions, so you can use them as a checklist. The first sentence gives you the core task. The second sentence reminds you what to look *at*:

- Line of reasoning
- Use of evidence

The third sentence reminds you what to look *for*:

- Questionable assumptions
- Alternative explanations or counterexamples

Finally, the fourth sentence reminds you about other stuff you can add to your essay.

Brainstorming Method 4: Remember Common Fallacies

In the sample essay prompts (and in Critical Reasoning arguments, for that matter), many of the same logical fallacies show up again and again. If you have trouble spotting flaws, review a list of these fallacies. You can find an extended list in the *Foundations of GMAT Verbal Strategy Guide*. Here's a condensed list with a few alterations:

1. **Alternative Causes**

    If the author asserts that X causes Y, what *else* could be the cause of Y?

    Correlation ≠ Causation: If X and Y happen at the same time, it's not necessarily true that X causes Y. It could be that Y causes X, or some Z causes them both, or they just randomly happened together on this one occasion.

    After ≠ Because: If Y happens *after* X, it's not necessarily true that Y happens *because of* X. Some other cause could be at work.

    Future ≠ Past: If X did cause Y in the past, will X always cause Y in the future? Not necessarily. Circumstances could change.

2. **Unforeseen Consequences**

    If the author proposes Plan A to achieve Goal B, what could go *wrong*?

    Nothing's Perfect: How could the plan fail to achieve the stated goal? Does it go too far or not far enough? What implementation challenges has the author overlooked?

    Isn't It Ironic: What bad side effects of the plan could happen? These side effects might be bad on their own, or they might directly prevent the plan from achieving its goal. Economic examples of the latter include customer attrition (if you raise prices to increase revenue, customers may flee) and price wars (if you cut your price to gain market share, your competition could cut prices in response). Think about who has been ignored by the author (such as customers and competitors) and what their negative responses to the plan might be.

Skill & Will: If people are involved in implementing the plan (and they always are), you need the people to have both the *skill* to succeed and the *will* to succeed. Do they? Who benefits from the plan, and are they the same people who need to carry it out?

3. Faulty Use of Evidence

What is sketchy about the evidence?

Limited Sample: Do you have too little data? How are the mentioned cases not representative of the wider world?

Troubled Analogy: If the author draws a conclusion about M from facts about "similar" N, how are M and N different? What differing conditions has the author ignored?

What It Really Means: The evidence simply may not imply what the author claims that it does.

4. Faulty Use of Language

What ***extreme*** words does the author use? What ***vague*** terms are in the argument? You may even encounter a math fallacy, such as an argument that makes assumptions about real quantities when only percents have been given.

Now that you have plenty of ideas about possible flaws (and how to brainstorm them), look at the flaws described in an example essay: the 6.0 essay in *The Official Guide for GMAT Review*. The given argument proposes an automatic early warning system to eliminate midair collisions between airplanes. Four flaws in this argument are pointed out in the second paragraph of the essay. Here's a brief list, as if they were brainstormed:

- Assumes cause of collisions = lack of knowledge
    - What if pilots don't pay attention to the warning system?
- Assumes pilots automatically obey the warning
    - What if they don't?
- Limited to commercial planes
    - What about other kinds of planes?
- What if the system fails?

The first two flaws are examples of the *skill & will* fallacy. The last two flaws are examples of *nothing's perfect*: the plan doesn't go far enough, and it ignores the possibility of failure.

Not every flaw in the argument is captured in the essay. That's fine! For instance, the author never criticizes the use of the extreme word "eliminate" in the conclusion ("reduce" would be more defensible). You can get a 6.0 on the essay without considering every last flaw in the argument.

Go ahead and brainstorm flaws in the Tarquinia argument. Take minutes and use any method you prefer in order to generate several specific flaws. Here is the prompt again; cover up the answers below the box until you have finished brainstorming.

> The country of Tarquinia has a much higher rate of traffic accidents per person than its neighbors, and in the vast majority of cases one or more drivers is found to be at fault in the courts. Therefore, Tarquinia should abolish driver-side seatbelts, airbags, and other safety measures that protect the driver, while new cars should be installed with a spike on the steering column pointed at the driver's heart. These measures will eliminate traffic accidents in Tarquinia by motivating drivers to drive safely.

Here are some examples of flaws in this argument:

• Higher accident rate = meaningful? – What if Tarquinia is not comparable to its neighbors? (car ownership, rural/urban mix might be different)	*Troubled Analogy*
• Guilt in courts = true guilt? – What if courts are bad or just bureaucratic? Ignores other factors.	*What It Really Means*

• Drivers have the capability to prevent all or most accidents. (Maybe it's always icy in Tarquinia.)
• Extreme punishment (fender bender = death)
  – Who will support, implement?
  – People would disable the system.
	Skill & Will

• Death spike applies only to new cars. – System only works if all cars are deadly to drivers.	*Nothing's Perfect*
• Who would buy new cars? No one!	*Isn't It Ironic*

On first reading the argument, you may have felt that the proposed measures were extreme. However, you aren't supposed to talk about whether *you* yourself agree with the plan.

Instead, imagine how other people and companies would react. It would be nearly impossible to get car manufacturers, dealers, and the rest of the population to stick to the plan.

MANHATTAN
PREP

How to Structure the Essay

A good GMAT essay has three parts:

1. Introduction
2. Body
3. Conclusion

How you structure the body can vary, but your introduction and conclusion will be structured fairly similarly regardless of the specific argument you're given.

Introduction

First, briefly restate the argument's main claim or conclusion; if the argument is a plan, state the plan. Do not simply quote the argument; put it into your own words to show that you understood it:

> The author proposes plan X to accomplish goal Y…

Next, introduce your thesis statement: the argument is fundamentally flawed in some serious way.

For example, the thesis of the 6.0 example essay in the *Official Guide* is as follows:

> *The argument … omits some important concerns that must be addressed to substantiate the argument.*

Notice how general this thesis is! The essay writer is saying in a fancy way that the argument doesn't work. Here are some other examples:

> *This plan is fundamentally flawed, in that the evidence provided fails to support the author's claim.*

> *The author makes several assumptions that are unlikely to be true, in which case her argument is seriously compromised.*

To bulk up the intro paragraph, mention one or two of the most egregious flaws you discovered. Don't go into detail; you'll do that in the body of the essay.

If you'd like to give a positive nod to the argument, do so *before* your thesis, using a concession word such as *although*:

> Although the argument has some merits, a number of defects undermine the claim … .

Body

Describe and justify 3–5 specific flaws from the argument. If you brainstormed more than 5 flaws, pick the best and drop the rest.

You can put all the flaws in one big paragraph, as the 6.0 example essay does. Describe each flaw in one sentence, then justify it in the next:

> The author fails to consider whether requiring death spikes in new cars will impact sales of new cars. If most potential customers decide to buy used cars instead, then most cars will not contain the death spikes, derailing part of the author's plan.
>
> The author's evidence also falls short of establishing that drivers are actually capable of avoiding all accidents. Drivers are found to be at fault in "the vast majority" of cases, not all of them. In addition, even when someone is found to be at fault legally, it is not necessarily the case that she or he could have prevented the accident by driving more carefully.

In this case, save your discussion of improvements for the conclusion.

Alternatively, you can put each flaw in a separate body paragraph. Introduce the flaw, justify it, and then discuss how the author could address the flaw. For example:

> The author's evidence falls short of establishing that drivers are actually capable of avoiding all accidents. Drivers are found to be at fault in "the vast majority" of cases, not all of them. At least some drivers, then, would be put to death through no fault of their own, surely not the intended consequence of this law. In addition, the author appears to fail to realize that the death spikes would be in both cars, so both the driver who caused the accident and the one who is the victim will be killed! Under those circumstances, the author may well achieve his stated goal, because it is unlikely that anyone will ever drive again.

You can even group a couple of flaws together in one paragraph, if they are related. For instance, you could make one body paragraph about *poor use of evidence* (with 2–3 flaws) and another about *faulty line of reasoning* (with another 2–3 flaws).

Conclusion

1. Restate briefly *that* the argument is flawed and recap *why* this is the case:

   In summary . . . .

2. Mention potential fixes to the line of reasoning used in the argument, if you haven't already:

   To address the problems in the argument, one would have to … (gather more data of XYZ kind) (run pilot projects to test the hypothesis) (etc.).

MANHATTAN
PREP

Use new language in your recap. You're saying, yet again, that the argument is flawed, but you need a novel way to say it. Replace particular words (e.g., flaw) with synonyms (error, gap, mistake, defect, fault, imperfection).

If you haven't already discussed possible improvements, do so here. If you are searching for still other things to say—and you have time—revisit the last sentence of the instructions. You can discuss possible new evidence or ways to evaluate the argument. Note that the 6.0 essay published in the *Official Guide* gives *very* short shrift to potential improvements. All the essay really does is explain the flaws; only the very last sentence gives a nod to fixes.

By the way, avoid humor in general; it can be easily misinterpreted in print. That said, don't be afraid to let your personality shine through, if that helps you generate the volume of content you need.

How to Vary Sentence Structure and Content

How could you improve this sample paragraph?

> The death spikes are one major flaw in the argument. Death spikes will only be installed in new cars. Only some drivers will have the ultimate incentive to avoid all accidents. Some people may even avoid buying new cars. The death spike may not be the deterrent that the author hopes.

The paragraph contains some good ideas, but the presentation of those ideas could be better. The sentences are pretty short, and three of the five use *death spikes* as the subject. The ideas aren't very well connected to each other, and the last sentence could use a transition word to indicate more clearly that it is summarizing the paragraph.

Take a look at this example:

> The author fails to consider the potential ramifications of the death spike plan. The spikes will only be installed in new cars, so only a subset of drivers will have the ultimate incentive to avoid all accidents, creating an imbalance among different drivers on the road. Some may counter that this drawback will disappear as more people buy new cars, but the death spike mandate may actually cause people to prefer used cars to new ones, perpetuating the imbalance long-term. In short, the death spike may not be the deterrent that the author hopes.

In the second example, the author combines some sentences in order to better connect the ideas and varies the structure so that the subjects aren't always the same. The author also adds modifiers to increase the complexity of the discussion and add nuance. Finally, the author uses a transition phrase, *in short*, to indicate that the last sentence summarizes the main point of the paragraph.

As you write, keep three aspects in mind:

1. A sentence should contain one clear, central thought.
2. Use modifiers to add complexity and nuance to the main thought.
3. Use signal words, such as *therefore*, *however*, and *in short* to signal transitions to the reader.

For more, read "Appendix A: How to Write Better Sentences" at the end of this book.

Sentence-by-Sentence Analysis of the 6.0 Essay

Let's examine each sentence in the 6.0 example essay in the *Official Guide*:

Paragraph 1, Sentence 1

The argument …	omits …	concerns
Subject	*Verb*	*Object*

To the core S–V–O structure, various modifiers are added, as you've already seen.

Paragraph 1, Sentence 2

The statement …	describes …	the system and [how it operates]
Subject	*Verb*	*Object*

The object is compound: *X and Y.* The second part of the object is known as a noun clause: a mini-sentence (*it operates*) with a word (*how*) that allows the whole thing to act like a noun in a bigger sentence. Instead, the author could have written an action noun: *its operation.* Either way is good enough. The noun clause *how it operates* is perhaps not as parallel to *the system* as you'd like, but the GMAT won't care about this minor degree of parallelism violation on the AWA.

Various modifiers are added, including an adverb (*simply*) and a subordinate clause (*that follows …*) that happens to contain another noun clause (*what this warning system will do*).

Paragraph 1, Sentence 3

This …	does not constitute …	an argument …, and	it …	does not provide …	support or proof
Subject	*Verb*	*Object*	*Subject*	*Verb*	*Object*

This sentence is compound: *full sentence, and full sentence.* The second object is compound (*or*). The word *This* without a noun following does not have a completely clear antecedent (the author seems to mean *the statement*, the subject of the prior sentence). Again, the AWA scorers are willing to accept minor grammatical blemishes of this kind. The compound core is fleshed out by a variety of modifiers.

MANHATTAN
PREP

Paragraph 2, Sentence 1

The argument …	does not address …	the cause …, the use …, or [who is involved …]
Subject	*Verb*	*Object*

The object is triply compound: *X*, *Y*, or *Z*. The third part is another noun clause—again, not as parallel as would be ideal, but remember that this essay got the top score.

An adverb is placed as a signal word at the start of the sentence: *Most conspicuously.* In that position, the adverb comments on the entire thought.

Paragraph 2, Sentence 2

The argument	assumes	that …
Subject	*Verb*	*Object*

	the cause	is	that …
	Subject	*Verb*	*Object*

	X, Y, and Z	are	A or B
	Subject	*Verb*	*Adjectives*

This sentence looks more complicated than it is. After a verb, what the word *that* does is allow you to embed a whole sentence as the object of the verb:

"My mother believes *that I am right.*"

What does my mother believe? She believes something: *that I am right.*

Having two levels (one outer and one inner) is totally fine. Three pushes the limit, as in the case above. Never go four levels deep: *My mother believes that the argument assumes that the cause is that…*

The most embedded level in the sentence has a triple-compound subject, connected by a linking verb (*are*) to two adjectives. Modifiers are sprinkled throughout (e.g., the signal word *First*).

This sentence loses its thread somewhat; it goes too deep and tries to pack too much in. Once again, remember that this essay earned a 6.0. You can get away with a few clunkers.

Paragraph 2, Sentence 3

The argument …	describes …	a system
Subject	*Verb*	*Object*

A variation that's new to this sentence is an opening modifier: *In a weak attempt to support its claim.* Occasionally throw in such a modifier, rather than lead with a bare subject or a simple signal word or phrase.

Paragraph 2, Sentence 4

But if	the cause …	is	that …
	Subject	*Verb*	*Object*

			pilots	are not paying	attention …,
			Subject	*Verb*	*Object*

	system …	will not solve	the problem
	Subject	*Verb*	*Object*

You're now encountering a sentence-level subordinate clause: *If [subordinate clause], main sentence.* The subordinate clause has one level of embedding: *the cause is that…*

The signal word *But* indicates a clear contrast to what's come before.

Paragraph 2, Sentence 5

The argument …	never addresses …	the interface … and [how this will affect …]
Subject	*Verb*	*Object*

The author continues to earn minor traffic violations: the two parts of the object are not as parallel as the GMAT would want in Sentence Correction, and the additional floating *this* could raise a grammarian's eyebrows. Your takeaway should be that your grammar need not be perfect on this essay. What's more important is the quality (and quantity) of your thinking.

The signal word *Second* broadcasts the essay writer's position in the list of flaws.

Paragraph 2, Sentence 6

If	the pilot or flight specialist …	does not conform …
	Subject	*Verb*

collisions …	will not be avoided
Subject	*Verb*

The second verb is in the passive voice, a completely appropriate choice.

Paragraph 2, Sentence 7

If	planes …	are involved …
	Subject	*Verb*

the problem …	cannot be solved …	by a system …

Subject	Verb	Agent

The passive voice is again used in the main clause. This time, the agent is indicated in the phrase *by a system*. The signal word *Finally* indicates that the list of flaws is wrapping up.

Paragraph 2, Sentence 8

The argument ...	does not address ...	[what would happen in the event that ...]
Subject	Verb	Object

The object is another noun clause (a form that the author evidently loves) with an embedded sentence inside (*the warning system collapses ...*). The author sneaks another flaw into the essay under the banner of the word *also*. In other words, *Finally* wasn't final, but this contradiction is negligible in the scheme of things.

Paragraph 3, Sentence 1

Because	the argument ...	leaves out ...	issues ...
	Subject	Verb	Object

it ...	is not ...	sound or persuasive
Subject	Verb	Adjectives

Some people believe that you cannot start a sentence with *Because*. You can, as long as you follow the *Because* clause with a main clause, as the author does correctly here. The word *it* has a clear antecedent (*the argument*).

Paragraph 3, Sentence 2

If	it ...	included ...	the items ...
	Subject	Verb	Object

the argument ...	would have been ...	more thorough and convincing
Subject	Verb	Adjectives

The pronoun *it* still clearly refers to *the argument* from the previous sentence.

Technically, the two clauses don't match in tense. Grammarians would say that you can write *If it included ... it would be ...* OR *If it had included ... it would have been ... .* Evidently, the AWA graders didn't care, in the end.

Sample Essay

Had enough sentence analysis? Itching to get on with it and *write*?

Here's the Tarquinia essay again. On your computer, open up a basic word processor (WordPad or NotePad), one that doesn't have any spelling or grammar check. Alternatively, open up Microsoft Word and disable automatic spell/grammar check.

Set a timer for 30 minutes and write your essay.

> The country of Tarquinia has a much higher rate of traffic accidents per person than its neighbors, and in the vast majority of cases one or more drivers is found to be at fault in the courts. Therefore, Tarquinia should abolish driver-side seatbelts, airbags, and other safety measures that protect the driver, while new cars should be installed with a spike on the steering column pointed at the driver's heart. These measures will eliminate traffic accidents in Tarquinia by motivating drivers to drive safely.

> Discuss how well reasoned you find this argument. In your discussion, be sure to analyze the line of reasoning and the use of evidence in the argument. For example, you may need to consider what questionable assumptions underlie the thinking and what alternative explanations or counterexamples might weaken the conclusion. You can also discuss what sort of evidence would strengthen or refute the argument, what changes in the argument would make it more logically sound, and what, if anything, would help you better evaluate its conclusion.

When you're done, cut and paste the results into Microsoft Word, so that you can do a word count. Recall that you're aiming for approximately 300 words and about 15 sentences, for an average of 20 or so words per sentence. If your essay has substantially fewer than 300 words or an average of 20 words per sentence, you'll need to bulk up.

Next, run the Spelling & Grammar checker. Note any errors and figure out how you could fix them.

Now take a look at a sample essay for the Tarquinia prompt:

> In response to the comparatively high rate of traffic accidents in Tarquinia, as well as to the results of court cases, the author argues that measures should be taken to compromise driver safety, in order to motivate safer driving. This argument suffers from a number of flaws, ranging from flimsy use of evidence to ill-conceived elements of the proposal, that would collectively mandate a full re-conception before the proposal could be carried out.
>
> First of all, the author cites two pieces of supporting evidence, which, even if true, should be challenged on the basis of their applicability. Tarquinia may have a higher rate of accidents than its neighbors, but what if those neighbors have vastly different circumstances? Rates of car ownership, highway safety conditions (even including weather), and urban/rural divides would need to be controlled for before reliable conclusions could be drawn. Likewise, it may be true that Tarquinian courts find one or more drivers guilty in most cases, but the degree to which these findings are driven by administrative necessity or other unrelated factors is unknown. Perhaps insurance law in the country demands that one or the other driver be found at fault, even if road conditions are largely to blame. These questions call the utility of the mentioned evidence into question.
>
> Secondly, the design of the plan is highly questionable from the standpoint of practicality, even without consideration of the moral implications. The first accidental fender bender that kills both drivers would likely cause the population of Tarquinia to reject the proposal as sadistic and extreme. Moreover, the fact that the proposal only applies to new cars creates another logical hole big enough to drive a truck through. No car buyer would purchase a new car willingly, and if any new cars did wind up on the road, the presence of old cars (which would not be subject to driver hazard) would undermine the self-enforcement regime, since not all drivers would be subject to the penalty of death by impalement for poor driving.
>
> In order to improve the proposal, the author would need to establish, first, that only those who are truly guilty of causing accidents might suffer the penalty of death. Second, the author would need to demonstrate that the residents of Tarquinia find these circumstances acceptable and will therefore accept the diminished safety regulations and, ultimately, change their driving behavior to eliminate traffic accidents.

Go line by line and compare how you expressed a point with how the above essay expressed a similar point. Borrow or steal whatever you find useful—word choices, phrasing, sentence or paragraph structure. How? Simply retype the words or sentences in question. By running them through your fingers, you start to make them your own.

While this essay is not perfect, it's likely good enough to get a 5.0 or higher. Good enough!

How to Prepare for the Essay

Now that you've gotten this far, do two more things to get ready:

1. Do GMAT Write.

GMAT Write is the gold standard, made by the makers of the GMAT itself. You practice with real prompts and are scored by the same computer algorithm as that used on the real exam.

You can purchase access to GMAT Write on the **mba.com** website. If you are a Manhattan Prep course student, you get a free coupon in your Student Center.

If your score comes back as a 4.5 or higher, rest easy. You just need to take one more step (#2 below). If your score comes back as a 3.5 or lower, see "Additional Preparation" below. Finally, if you get a 4.0, you're on the cusp. You might want to put more time into preparation, but you might be able to skate by without it.

2. Do the Argument Essay section on all of your practice CATs.

The full GMAT takes a little over 3.5 hours, so you need to practice your mental stamina. In addition, you want to make sure that your practice scores reflect your full current scoring capability. If you have more mental energy for the Quant and Verbal sections because you skipped one or both of the earlier sections, your scores are likely to be artificially inflated.

Additional Preparation

If you have scored a 3.5 or lower on GMAT Write or on the real AWA—or you think you will—you need to put more time into preparing for the essay.

Here are practical steps to take:

Step 1: Work through the *Foundations of GMAT Verbal Strategy Guide Supplement.*

You may already be spending time with that book. Great—now you have another reason to focus. *Foundations of GMAT Verbal* covers all three Verbal question types (Sentence Correction, Critical Reasoning, and Reading Comprehension), all of which come into play on the AWA essay. You need the parts of speech and other grammatical principles to strengthen the sentences you write. You need to spot missing assumptions and analyze other logical flaws to write an effective essay about a flawed argument. Finally, the better you *read* this kind of text (as in an RC passage), the better you can *write* this kind of text.

MANHATTAN
PREP

So focus on Verbal basics to build skill for the essay.

Step 2: Read and write summaries of high-quality articles in English.

Find good source material. Use publications such as the *Economist*, the *Smithsonian*, the *Atlantic*, and the *New Yorker*. For daily newspapers, try the *New York Times*, the *Wall Street Journal*, the *Washington Post*, and the *Financial Times*. Go get *Scientific American*, the *Journal of American History*, the *Harvard Business Review*, or the *McKinsey Quarterly*. Pick up an alumni magazine from a top university. Visit aldaily.com for links to wonderful "Arts and Letters" pieces from across the web.

Take note of sentences that strike you. Pick apart the core and examine how the author added modifiers or other bits of nuance and richness to the sentence. If you spot a particularly great sentence, you may even want to recopy it to solidify it in your brain.

If you get really ambitious, you can *rewrite* a piece, summarizing it or playing with language in some other way.

Step 3: Do a few sample essays from the *Official Guide*.

Pick a prompt at random. Give yourself 30 minutes and type an essay into a bare-bones word processor, as described earlier.

Now, without the pressure of time, analyze and rewrite each sentence in your essay. How could you have phrased your thought more precisely and more expressively? What words could you have chosen differently? How would you restructure the sentence?

At first, focus on polishing only the ideas that you were able to generate under time pressure. This way, the next time you have similar thoughts (as you will on other essays), the corresponding sentences will more easily and quickly coalesce.

Now look for small gaps that you could close by adding material. Could you bulk up any existing sentences? What additional refinements could you add as modifiers? Could you provide better navigation and logical flow with signal words?

Finally, look for big gaps and other wholesale alterations. Did you miss any key flaws in the argument? If so, which kinds? Write and polish sentences corresponding to these flaws. Is there anything you'd cut or otherwise change drastically? If so, what?

Step 4: Learn to type faster.

The faster and more easily you can type, the less brainpower that goes into typing—and the more that goes into your thinking and writing. If you type slowly, then your brain runs far ahead of your fingers, and you lose your train of thought. In contrast, if you can get your thoughts down in near real time, you will simply write better.

Longer essays get higher scores, by and large. But that's far from the only reason to learn to type for real. We're talking about transforming your life. If you spend more than 20 minutes a day at a computer keyboard, the time you invest in learning to type quickly by touch (without looking at the keys) will pay off more than any other investment you could possibly make.

Take a touch-typing course. There are a zillion free resources on the web. Google "learn to type" and see what you find.

Finally, if all goes awry on test day, there *is* an AWA rescoring service on **mba.com**. For $45, you can get your essay rescored; contact GMAT Customer Service. Be advised, however, that you are unlikely to see an increase. Only even consider rescoring if *all* of the following conditions hold:

- You scored a 3.5 or lower on the real AWA.
- You scored a 4.5 or higher on GMAT Write.
- After honest and thorough reflection, you feel that you wrote a much better essay than your score indicates.

If you pay appropriate time and attention to the essay section before test day, you're unlikely to find yourself in this position.

Chapter *of* 3

Integrated Reasoning

Introduction to
Integrated Reasoning

In This Chapter...

Chapter 3

Introduction to Integrated Reasoning

The Integrated Reasoning (IR) section of the GMAT launched in June 2012, replacing one of the two essays at the beginning of the test. The sections of the GMAT are shown below:

GMAT

Essay	*30 min*	*0 – 6*
IR	*30 min*	*1 – 8*
Quant *37 questions*	*75 min*	*0 – 51* *subscore*
Verbal *41 questions*	*75 min*	*0 – 51* *subscore*

Overall
200 – 800

As the name implies, Integrated Reasoning asks you to do both math and verbal thinking as you answer 12 questions based on approximately 10 prompts, or sets of information for you to analyze. Most prompts and questions have formats unique to this section of the test: fill-in-the-blank statements, true/false statements, and other multiple-part questions.

IR is scored separately from the rest of the test. Your IR score does not affect your score on any other section, though the mental effort you spend on IR could affect your ability to perform well later in the test. The IR score goes from 1 to 8 in whole-number increments. As with the Quant and Verbal sections of the GMAT, you must answer IR questions in the order they appear (that is, you cannot skip forward or go back). Unlike the Quant and Verbal sections of the GMAT, however, the IR section is *not* adaptive and therefore your score is primarily driven by how many of the 12 questions you answer correctly, with slight adjustments for differences in question difficulty.

Because the IR section is relatively new, there is not yet a consensus as to how much weight to give the score during the admissions process. Most schools are either not using the score yet or weighting it only lightly in their admissions decisions. Schools that are using the score seem to be concentrating only on high or low scores: a 7 or an 8 is a plus for your application, while a 3 or lower is a minus. An in-between score is neither a hindrance nor a help.

The IR score is likely to increase in importance over time, as the admission officers gain more data to determine how much weight to place on the score. For now, aim to score a 5 or a 6 and save most of your mental energy for the Quant and Verbal sections. (Unless, of course, you find the IR section relatively easy, in which case go for a higher score!)

Most business schools use case studies to teach some or even most topics. Cases are true histories of difficult business situations; they include vast amounts of real information, both quantitative and verbal, that you must sort through and analyze to glean insights and make decisions.

The IR section is designed to mirror two key aspects of case analysis that the Quant and Verbal sections of the GMAT fail to accomplish:

1. Math–verbal integration
2. The flood of real-world data

Problems on the Quant section of the test typically give you only what you need in order to solve, and no more; the numbers often simplify cleanly, leaving you with an integer solution. In addition, though you do need to translate words into math, the Quant section does not incorporate logical reasoning or other Verbal skills. On the verbal side of things, while Critical Reasoning (CR) and Reading Comprehension (RC) questions do include some extraneous information, they require only light mathematical understanding on rare occasions.

In contrast, Integrated Reasoning gives you giant tables of ugly numbers, many of which you'll never actually use. Further, you'll have to integrate these numbers with the kind of reasoning and analysis typically found on the Verbal section of the GMAT.

In short, the GMAT seeks to measure your ability to do case analysis in business school by giving you mini-case analyses on the IR section.

But there is a key reason not to stress too much: IR tests the same core skills as the rest of the test, just with a twist. By preparing for the main event of the GMAT, you're already preparing for IR!

The Four Types of Problems

An Integrated Reasoning section contains a total of 12 questions associated with approximately 10 prompts.

A prompt is the collection of information you'll use to answer the question(s). Think of the Verbal section of the GMAT: a Reading Comprehension passage is a prompt and this prompt is accompanied by three or four questions.

There are four types of IR prompts. A typical section consists of one Multi-Source Reasoning prompt (with three associated questions), two Table prompts, three Graphical Interpretation prompts, and four Two-Part Analysis prompts, though the exact mix can vary.

3

Multi-Source Reasoning

Multi-Source Reasoning (MSR) prompts are the closest equivalent to Reading Comprehension on the Verbal section, in which large passages of text are accompanied by a set of questions based on that text. Unlike RC passages, however, the information in MSR can include tables, charts, or other diagrams along with the text, and all of the information provided is spread across two or three tabs that must be viewed one at a time. In order to answer the accompanying questions, you must integrate information from across the different tabs.

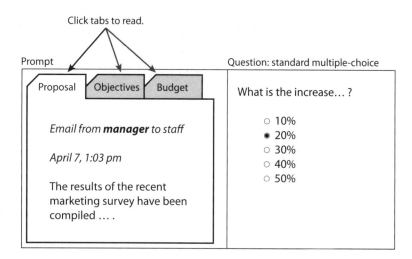

As with RC prompts, MSR prompts will typically come with three questions, one of which will likely be a typical multiple-choice question with five answers. The other two questions will likely be opposite-answer questions (e.g., true/false, yes/no).

An opposite-answer question will present you with three yes/no or true/false (or similar) statements; in order to answer the question correctly, you'll have to answer all three parts correctly. In other words, no partial credit is given for answering only a portion of a problem correctly.

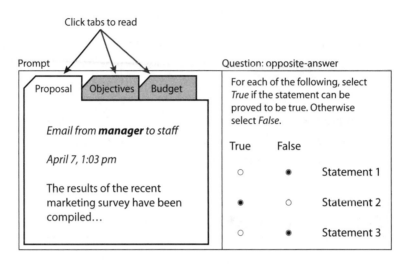

You'll learn more about MSR problems in Chapter 4.

Table Analysis

The Table Analysis (Table) prompt is a sortable table that might be accompanied by a blurb giving you context about the information contained in the table. The blurb can be quite basic (for instance, a title); other times, the blurb may contain information crucial to your ability to answer questions.

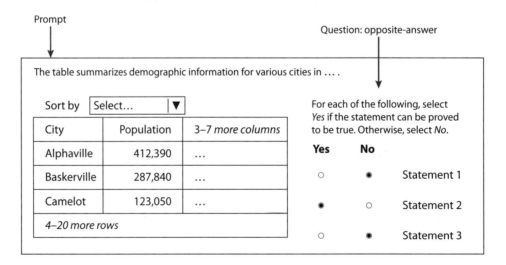

MANHATTAN
PREP

Table prompts will be accompanied by a single opposite-answer question with three yes/no or true/false (or similar) statements. Again, to answer the question correctly you'll have to answer all three parts correctly; all multi-part questions on the IR section require you to answer all parts correctly in order to earn credit for that problem.

You'll learn more about Table problems in chapter 5.

Graphics Interpretation

Graphics Interpretation (Graph) prompts will present you with some kind of a graph—anything from a classic pie chart or bar graph to some kind of unusual diagram that you may not have seen before.

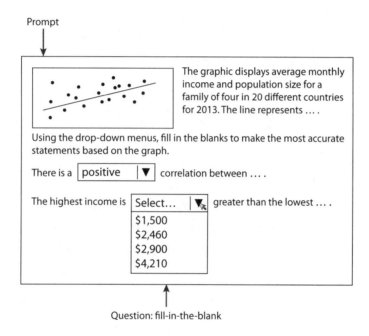

Prompt

The graphic displays average monthly income and population size for a family of four in 20 different countries for 2013. The line represents … .

Using the drop-down menus, fill in the blanks to make the most accurate statements based on the graph.

There is a [positive ▼] correlation between … .

The highest income is [Select... ▼] greater than the lowest … .

$1,500
$2,460
$2,900
$4,210

Question: fill-in-the-blank

Graph problems will be accompanied by a two-part fill-in-the-blank question. You'll be given one or two sentences with two drop-down menus placed somewhere in the text, offering you multiple choice options to fill in the blanks. As with earlier question types, the only way to answer the question correctly is to answer both parts correctly.

You'll learn more about Graphs in Chapter 6.

Two-Part Analysis

Superficially, Two-Part Analysis (Two-Part) prompts will look the most like multiple-choice questions from the Quant and Verbal sections of the test—until you get to the answers.

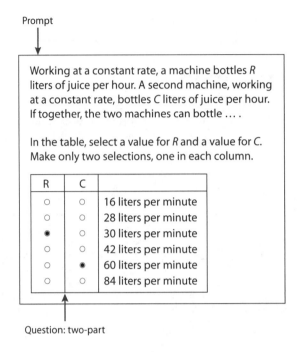

Prompt

Working at a constant rate, a machine bottles R liters of juice per hour. A second machine, working at a constant rate, bottles C liters of juice per hour. If together, the two machines can bottle … .

In the table, select a value for R and a value for C. Make only two selections, one in each column.

R	C	
○	○	16 liters per minute
○	○	28 liters per minute
●	○	30 liters per minute
○	○	42 liters per minute
○	●	60 liters per minute
○	○	84 liters per minute

Question: two-part

The above example fairly closely resembles a standard Quant question, though as the name implies, you'll have to answer a Two-Part question (one in each column). Notice that the answer choices are the same for both questions. As with all other multi-part questions, you'll need to answer both parts correctly in order to earn credit on this question.

Two-Part prompts involve the least amount of math–verbal integration, and tend to be primarily quant-based, verbal-based, or logic-based.

You'll learn more about Two-Part problems in Chapter 7.

IR Connections to Quant and Verbal

The Integrated Reasoning section tests some of the same facts and skills tested on other sections of the GMAT.

Quant

Though any part of GMAT Quant is fair game on the IR section of the test, IR does emphasize two main content areas:

1. Decimals, Percents, & Ratios
2. Statistics

MANHATTAN
PREP

For both Quant and IR, you'll need to know the same formulas, facts, and rules. The general problem-solving techniques you learn for the Quant section will also work on the IR section.

You can find an overview of the two main Quant content areas in Appendix B of this guide. For more in-depth study of decimals, percents, and ratios, see the *Fractions, Decimals, & Percents GMAT Strategy Guide*. For more in-depth study of statistics, see the *Word Problems GMAT Strategy Guide*.

A basic, on-screen calculator is available during the Integrated Reasoning section (but *not* during the Quant section). The calculator can be a blessing and a curse; it's important to learn when and how to use this tool (and when not to use it).

In the test screen window, click the link in the upper left corner to pull up the calculator. Note that the calculator will float above the problem on the screen; you can move it around, but you cannot click on the problem to answer the question while the calculator is still open.

The calculator will include the following, fairly limited functions:

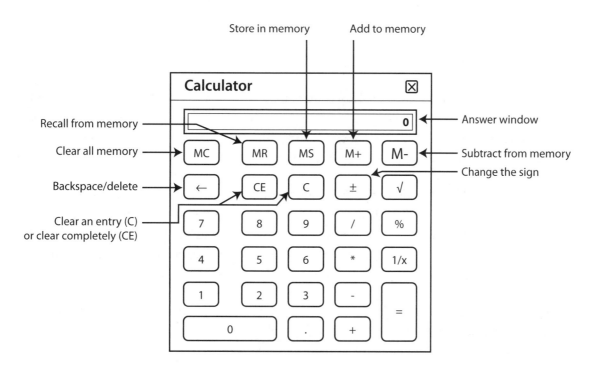

Have you ever panicked on a math question during a test, picked up a calculator, and punched in some numbers, hoping inspiration would strike? If you ever find yourself doing this during the IR section, stop immediately, pick an answer, and move on. The calculator is not a substitute for the actual solution process.

That said, don't hesitate to pull up the calculator when you do need it. The Quant section of the test often provides numbers that work pretty cleanly in calculations; the IR section, by contrast, won't hesitate to give you messy numbers. As long as you know what steps you want to take, the calculator will be a very helpful tool.

Verbal

The IR and Verbal sections overlap on reasoning and comprehension skills; the IR section does not include any grammar.

Some IR questions will look very similar to CR questions. For instance, an IR question may ask you to strengthen or weaken an argument. Inference questions are also quite common to CR, RC, and IR questions, and you can use many of the same techniques that you use to tackle these question types in CR and RC. However, the standard for CR and RC inferences is more strict: you must be able to prove the inference true from the text. In contrast, IR inference questions may involve some real world assumptions.

Scoring and Timing

As mentioned earlier in this chapter, the IR section of the test is not adaptive. That is, the questions will not get easier or harder based on your performance during the section. The questions are also not necessarily presented in order of difficulty, so do expect to hit harder questions in the middle of the section while there are still easier questions waiting for you later in the section.

As in the Quant and Verbal sections, the IR section requires you to answer the question on screen in order to get to the next question. In addition, you cannot return to a question once you have answered it. Because you may still have some easier questions waiting for you later in the section, it is very important not to get so caught up in one problem that you cannot get to the remaining questions.

The IR section has a time limit of 30 minutes. Because there are 12 questions total, you have an average of 2.5 minutes per question—if you try to answer them all. Unless you find IR easy, though, you're going to guess on at least one question in the section.

As you work through the test, you will earn points based upon the number of full questions you answer correctly. You must answer a multi-part question completely correctly to earn the point for that question. While the exact scoring scale has never been published, research has uncovered the fact that you can answer a number of questions incorrectly and still earn a good score on the test.

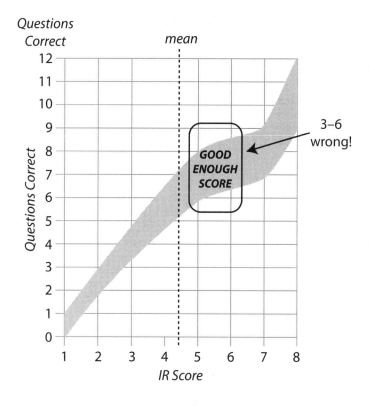

If you're going for a score of 6 or higher, plan to guess on 2 questions in the section. You'll be able to spend an average of 3 minutes on the remaining 10 questions, and you'll be able to answer some of these incorrectly and still hit your target score.

If you're going for a score of 5, plan to guess on three questions in the section. You'll have nearly 3.5 minutes to spend on the remaining nine questions. Likewise, you'll be able to answer some incorrectly and still hit the target.

By the time you're done studying for IR, you should know two things:

1. Your weakest question type(s)
2. Your target score

You'll guess—either twice or three times, depending on your target score—when you see harder questions in your weaker areas.

You'll learn more in Chapter 8 about how and when to guess, but while you study, keep in mind that you need to have a good handle on your own strengths and weaknesses in order to make good decisions about when to guess. (This is true for the whole test!)

How to Tackle IR: Understand–Plan–Solve (UPS)

Here is a universal four-step process for Integrated Reasoning:

Step 1:   Understand the prompt.

Step 2:   Understand the question.

Step 3:   Plan your approach.

Step 4:   Solve the problem.

At first glance, the process might seem pretty simple. Most test-takers, though, pay minimal attention to the first three steps. If you want to get through IR with a minimum of stress and a good score, follow the process!

Step 1: Understand the prompt.
Don't be so quick to jump to the solution process that you fail to thoroughly comprehend the given information. As you scan the given data, ask yourself *What* and *So what* questions:

What is this?
- What is the title or accompanying text indicating?
- What is in this tab, this row, or this column?
- What do these points on the graph represent?
- What kind of graph is this—column, line, bubble, etc.?
- What kind of numbers are these—percents, ranks, or absolute quantities, such as dollars or barrels?

So what about this?
- How is this information organized?
- Why is this part here? What purpose does it serve, relative to everything else?
- How does it all fit together? Draw connections.

Step 2: Understand the question.
Articulate the question to yourself in your own words before you try to solve it. The wording is sometimes meant to trick you. For instance, the question might imply that you must use an advanced, time-consuming technique, when a much faster shortcut exists.

Some people like to read the question first, before reading the prompt. If you like to do this, feel free to swap steps 1 and 2, as long as you don't skip either one!

Step 3: Plan your approach.

Next, you'll need to figure out what to *do* with the prompt in order to answer the question:

- What do you have to look up? Which portions should you re-read?

- What pieces of information do you have to combine?

- What formulas will you need to use?

- What shortcuts can you use? Can you estimate on any of the math?

You won't be able to determine every last step of your plan before you start to solve, but do think about the kind of information you need or the types of calculations you will need to do.

Step 4: Solve the problem.

Now execute your plan of attack. If you've done the first three steps well, solving should be pretty straightforward. Of course, you still need to take care. Be methodical and write notes and calculations clearly to minimize the chance of careless mistakes. Finally, if you get stuck at any step along the way, don't dwell. Go back and try to unstick yourself once. If you're still stuck, guess and move on to the next question.

Don't Let IR Mess Up the Rest of Your Test

Unfortunately, for many people, the Integrated Reasoning section is much harder than the Issue essay that it replaces.

If you try to do IR to the utmost of your ability, you will use up a lot of your mental stamina—with the Quant and Verbal sections still to come. You don't want to ace IR if that's going to cost you points on Quant and Verbal. Here's what to do:

- *Unless you find IR relatively easy, don't aim for a top score.* As of now, the Quant and Verbal sections are still more important than the IR section.

- *Build stamina in advance.* Take all practice exams under 100% official conditions, including the Analytical Writing Assessment essay and IR sections. Limit yourself to two 8-minute breaks, just like the real thing.

- *Know your strengths and weaknesses.* Skip two or three of the hardest (for you) questions. Study the solution techniques so that you can solve the ones that you do answer in the fastest and easiest way possible.

- *Replenish your brain's food.* During the break after IR, eat something containing protein, fat, and complex carbohydrates (a sandwich on whole grain bread, perhaps). During the break after Quant, drink glucose to help your brain counter mental fatigue; the sugar will give you a boost until the test is over. (Don't drink lots of glucose before then or your brain will crash before the test is over.) Fresh fruit or vegetable juice and coconut water are good sources of glucose.

Next, you'll transition to the Quant and Verbal sections of the test. Make a few small, but critical, adjustments and you'll be ready to go!

GMAT Quant

- *Don't ignore any information.* IR includes lots of extra information, but you'll need to use everything that a Quant problem tells you.

- *Think about how to set up the calculation in the easiest possible way.* On IR, you can use the calculator; on Quant, everything has to be done by hand. Luckily, the Quant problems that have "ugly" numbers can be solved via estimation or some other shortcut.

GMAT Verbal

- *Stop reading so carefully between the lines.* Some Verbal section questions do ask you to infer, but you're held to the standard of inferring what must be true from the given information. The IR section holds a looser standard, allowing you to infer what is plausible, though not necessarily definitely true.

Chapter 4 *of*
Integrated Reasoning

Multi-Source Reasoning

In This Chapter...

Chapter 4
Multi-Source Reasoning

Multi-Source Reasoning (MSR) prompts are similar to Reading Comprehension (RC) passages, with two key differences: MSR can include mathematical data, graphics, and tables along with the text, and the information provided will be split across two or three tabs.

Much like RC passages, the MSR prompt will appear on the left side of the screen, and the (typically) three accompanying questions will appear on the right side of the screen, one at a time. These questions are of two different types: multiple-choice and opposite-answer.

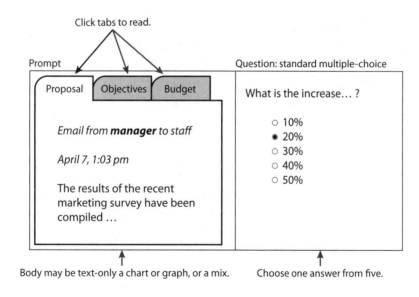

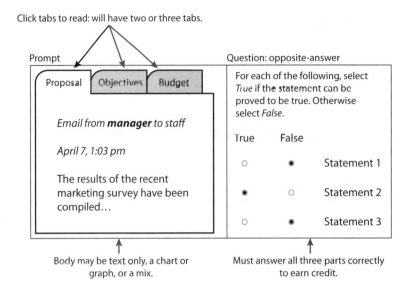

Click tabs to read: will have two or three tabs.

Prompt   Question: opposite-answer

Proposal   Objectives   Budget

For each of the following, select *True* if the statement can be proved to be true. Otherwise select *False*.

Email from **manager** to staff

April 7, 1:03 pm

The results of the recent marketing survey have been compiled…

	True	False	
	○	●	Statement 1
	●	○	Statement 2
	○	●	Statement 3

Body may be text only, a chart or graph, or a mix.

Must answer all three parts correctly to earn credit.

4

Most MSR questions will include one standard multiple-choice question and two opposite-answer questions (e.g., true/false, yes/no), though the exact question mix and number can vary.

The vast majority of questions will require you to integrate information from two of the tabs (and sometimes all three!).

How to Tackle MSR

As discussed in Chapter 3, "Introduction to Integrated Reasoning," you'll use the UPS process (Understand–Plan–Solve) to solve all IR problems, including MSR. UPS stands for understand the prompt, understand the question, plan, and solve. (If you skipped that chapter, you may want to go back and read the How to Tackle IR section.)

Step 1: Understand the prompt.

Take a look at the below two-tabbed MSR prompt. Here's the first tab:

Sales Breakout | Vitamin Content

E-mail from Purchasing Supervisor to Sales Manager:

Total April sales for your produce stand were $4,441; the itemized data is below.

We already know that customers base their purchasing decisions on whether something is in season and how much it costs. Management believes that customers also care about the health factor, such as how high the vitamin content is for different types of produce. Do you have any data that could help us to evaluate this question?

We also need to think about pricing strategies in light of the fact that some items have a far longer shelf life. Potatoes will last weeks in cold storage, while the tomatoes won't last more than a few days without suffering a reduction in quality. Please send me any information you have about spoilage rates or other factors we should consider when setting prices.

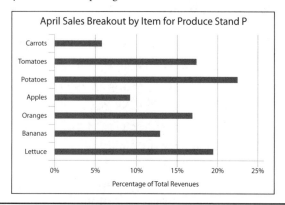

Here's the second tab:

Sales Breakout | **Vitamin Content**

E-mail from Sales Manager to Purchasing Supervisor:

Carrots, apples, and potatoes last a very long time in cold storage. I am a bit concerned about the lettuce, though; our farmers generally produce a higher volume of lettuce than of any other single item. The other items generally sell within acceptable time frames, even the tomatoes and bananas.

Customers do sometimes ask about the vitamin and nutrient content of various items. Maybe I should post the data on the pricing signs? Here's some data on the vitamin A and vitamin C content of our produce:

Vitamin Content of Produce Items Sold at Produce Stand P in April		
	Vitamin C Content	*Vitamin A Content*
Apples	low	low
Bananas	medium	low
Carrots	low	high
Lettuce	high	low
Oranges	high	medium
Potatoes	medium	low
Tomatoes	high	high

I also have research indicating that organic produce has a higher vitamin content than non-organic counterparts. I think that could be a very valuable marketing point.

In general, start with the first tab first and proceed through the remaining tabs in order. As you read, you are going to jot down information on your scrap paper, but you are not going to try to answer the questions from your notes. Rather, your **tab map** will help you figure out where to go in order to answer the various questions.

Glance at the tab titles first and use these to begin labeling your tab map: *Sales* and *Vitamin*. (It's okay that you don't yet understand the significance of these two words.) Then dive into the first tab, jot down what the passage says, and think about the "So what?": why does the passage say that?

Sales
    (What?)   April sales $4,441
                   Customers care: in season, cost, maybe vitamin?
                   Shelf life, spoilage rates vary. Pricing?
                   Graph: sales by item

So what? The next tab will presumably address the vitamin question, since that one is called *Vitamin Content*. Also, there are concerns about shelf life; the supervisor seems to be thinking that they might have to reduce prices on certain items with a shorter shelf life in order to make sure they sell before they spoil (though she doesn't actually say this). Finally, the opening paragraph provides an overall sales figure and the bar graph provides the percentage of sales by item; there may be some calculations coming soon. (Note: think this; don't actually write it out.)

Vitamin
    (What?)   Lettuce may be a problem; others fine
                   Some customers care about vitamins.
                   Organic
                   Table: vitamins A and C

So what? It sounds like lettuce might have spoilage/shelf-life issues, though the sales manager doesn't explicitly say so. Then there's a bunch of data on vitamin content; ignore that until you get a question about it. Finally, the last couple of sentences introduce the idea of organic produce. Since this wasn't mentioned anywhere earlier, you can jot down just the word *organic* and know exactly where to go if you get a question about that.

Take a moment to think about how the two tabs connect. The supervisor asks some questions and the manager responds to those questions. The two visuals contain the same list of fruits and vegetables, though not in the same order. It isn't clear at this point how the sales data and the vitamin content data might otherwise connect, so wait to see what questions you're asked.

Step 2: Understand the question.

Here are the two tabs again, along with the first question:

Sales Breakout	**Vitamin Content**

E-mail from Purchasing Supervisor to Sales Manager:

Total April sales for your produce stand were $4,441; the itemized data is below.

We already know that customers base their purchasing decisions on whether something is in season and how much it costs. Management believes that customers also care about the health factor, such as how high the vitamin content is for different types of produce. Do you have any data that could help us to evaluate this question?

We also need to think about pricing strategies in light of the fact that some items have a far longer shelf life. Potatoes will last weeks in cold storage, while the tomatoes won't last more than a few days without suffering a reduction in quality. Please send me any information you have about spoilage rates or other factors we should consider when setting prices.

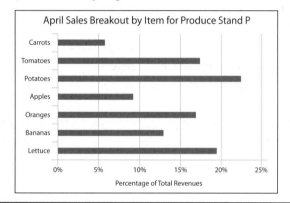

April Sales Breakout by Item for Produce Stand P

Sales Breakout	**Vitamin Content**

E-mail from Sales Manager to Purchasing Supervisor:

Carrots, apples, and potatoes last a very long time in cold storage. I am a bit concerned about the lettuce, though; our farmers generally produce a higher volume of lettuce than of any other single item. The other items generally sell within acceptable time frames, even the tomatoes and bananas.

Customers do sometimes ask about the vitamin and nutrient content of various items. Maybe I should post the data on the pricing signs? Here's some data on the vitamin A and vitamin C content of our produce:

Vitamin Content of Produce Items Sold at Produce Stand P in April		
	Vitamin C Content	*Vitamin A Content*
Apples	low	low
Bananas	medium	low
Carrots	low	high
Lettuce	high	low
Oranges	high	medium
Potatoes	medium	low
Tomatoes	high	high

I also have research indicating that organic produce has a higher vitamin content than non-organic counterparts. I think that could be a very valuable marketing point.

For each of the following, select *Justified* if it is a justified inference on the basis of the information provided. Otherwise, select *Not Justified*.

Justified	Not Justified	
○	○	Some of Produce Stand P's lettuce may spoil or be in danger of spoiling before it is all sold.
○	○	More bananas than apples are sold at Produce Stand P.
○	○	Produce high in vitamin A, vitamin C, or both accounted for more than half of April sales at Produce Stand P.

This is an opposite-answer question. These questions will always contain two "opposite" answers, such as true/false, yes/no, or, as in this case, justified/not justified. Three statements will accompany the question; your task is to choose a single answer for each statement. In order to earn credit for this question, you have to answer all three statements correctly.

This question specifically asks whether the statement is a *justified inference*. These statements will not be found directly in the passage; rather, you will have to determine whether something is reasonably justified based upon related information from the passage.

Next, scan through the three statements. On some problems, the statements are very similar and can be solved simultaneously or very similarly. On others, the statements are independent and must be solved separately.

In this case, the statements each address different aspects of the information provided, so work through them individually. Here's the first statement:

Justified	Not Justified	
○	○	Some of Produce Stand P's lettuce may spoil or be in danger of spoiling before it is all sold.

This statement talks about lettuce spoilage. Where do you need to go to find this information?

MANHATTAN
PREP

Step 3: Plan your approach.

Sales Breakout | **Vitamin Content**

E-mail from Purchasing Supervisor to Sales Manager:

Total April sales for your produce stand were $4,441; the itemized data is below.

We already know that customers base their purchasing decisions on whether something is in season and how much it costs. Management believes that customers also care about the health factor, such as how high the vitamin content is for different types of produce. Do you have any data that could help us to evaluate this question?

We also need to think about pricing strategies in light of the fact that some items have a far longer shelf life. Potatoes will last weeks in cold storage, while the tomatoes won't last more than a few days without suffering a reduction in quality. Please send me any information you have about spoilage rates or other factors we should consider when setting prices.

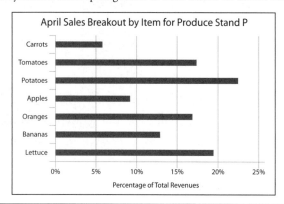

Sales Breakout | **Vitamin Content**

E-mail from Sales Manager to Purchasing Supervisor:

Carrots, apples, and potatoes last a very long time in cold storage. I am a bit concerned about the lettuce, though; our farmers generally produce a higher volume of lettuce than of any other single item. The other items generally sell within acceptable time frames, even the tomatoes and bananas.

Customers do sometimes ask about the vitamin and nutrient content of various items. Maybe I should post the data on the pricing signs? Here's some data on the vitamin A and vitamin C content of our produce:

Vitamin Content of Produce Items Sold at Produce Stand P in April		
	Vitamin C Content	**Vitamin A Content**
Apples	low	low
Bananas	medium	low
Carrots	low	high
Lettuce	high	low
Oranges	high	medium
Potatoes	medium	low
Tomatoes	high	high

I also have research indicating that organic produce has a higher vitamin content than non-organic counterparts. I think that could be a very valuable marketing point.

The *Sales* tab mentioned spoilage and the *Vitamin* tab specifically mentioned lettuce, so you'll need both to answer the question. Find and re-read the relevant text:

> (Sales Tab): *We also need to think about pricing strategies in light of the fact that some items have a far longer shelf life. Potatoes will last weeks in cold storage, while the tomatoes won't last more than a few days without suffering a reduction in quality. Please send me any information you have about spoilage rates or other factors we should consider when setting prices.*

> (Vitamin Tab) *Carrots, apples, and potatoes last a very long time in cold storage. I am a bit concerned about the lettuce, though; our farmers generally produce a higher volume of lettuce than of any other single item. The other items generally sell within acceptable time frames, even the tomatoes and bananas.*

Step 4: Solve the problem.

The supervisor points out that some items will last much longer than others, then asks about spoilage rates, implying that some items may spoil or be in danger of spoiling. The sales manager indicates that certain items do last a long time, but he is *concerned about the lettuce.* He also indicates that the *other items generally sell within acceptable time frames,* implying that the lettuce may be in danger of not selling within an acceptable time frame, or spoiling before it can be sold. This statement, then, is *Justified.*

Evaluate the second and third statements in the same manner, repeating steps two through four.

Justified	Not Justified	
O	O	More bananas than apples are sold at Produce Stand P.

Careful! The bar graph in the *Sales Breakout* shows information about sales revenues, not sales volume. While it is true that banana sales revenues were higher than apple sales revenues, the prompt does not indicate the relative number of items sold. This statement is *Not Justified.*

Justified	Not Justified	
O	O	Produce high in vitamin A, vitamin C, or both accounted for more than half of April sales at Produce Stand P.

The *Vitamin Content* has the vitamin data; the *Sales Breakout* has the sales data. You're going to have to combine the two tabs. First, go to *Vitamin Content* and write down the items that are high in either of the vitamins (or both): carrots, lettuce, oranges, and tomatoes. Next, click on the *Sales Breakout* and find the percentage of revenue for each item. Carrots and tomatoes are next to each other; together, they account for about 6 plus 17%, which sums to 23% of revenues. Oranges account for approximately 17% of revenues and lettuce for approximately 19%—more than enough to cross the 50% threshold. Therefore, this statement is *justified.*

The answers are as follows:

Justified	Not Justified	
◉	○	Some of Produce Stand P's lettuce may spoil or be in danger of spoiling before it is all sold.
○	◉	More bananas than apples are sold at Produce Stand P.
◉	○	Produce high in vitamin A, vitamin C, or both accounted for more than half of April sales at Produce Stand P.

Here is a second question for the same prompt; try out the UPS process yourself.

In the month of April, Produce Stand P generated approximately how much revenue, in dollars, from items that were high in both vitamin A and vitamin C content?

(A) $ 775
(B) $1,280
(C) $1,575
(D) $2,080
(E) $2,875

Sales Breakout | Vitamin Content

E-mail from Purchasing Supervisor to Sales Manager:

Total April sales for your produce stand were $4,441; the itemized data is below.

We already know that customers base their purchasing decisions on whether something is in season and how much it costs. Management believes that customers also care about the health factor, such as how high the vitamin content is for different types of produce. Do you have any data that could help us to evaluate this question?

We also need to think about pricing strategies in light of the fact that some items have a far longer shelf life. Potatoes will last weeks in cold storage, while the tomatoes won't last more than a few days without suffering a reduction in quality. Please send me any information you have about spoilage rates or other factors we should consider when setting prices.

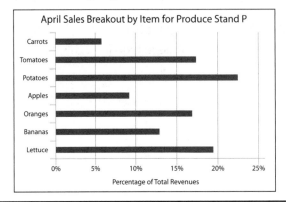

Sales Breakout | **Vitamin Content**

E-mail from Sales Manager to Purchasing Supervisor:

Carrots, apples, and potatoes last a very long time in cold storage. I am a bit concerned about the lettuce, though; our farmers generally produce a higher volume of lettuce than of any other single item. The other items generally sell within acceptable time frames, even the tomatoes and bananas.

Customers do sometimes ask about the vitamin and nutrient content of various items. Maybe I should post the data on the pricing signs? Here's some data on the vitamin A and vitamin C content of our produce:

Vitamin Content of Produce Items Sold at Produce Stand P in April		
	Vitamin C Content	*Vitamin A Content*
Apples	low	low
Bananas	medium	low
Carrots	low	high
Lettuce	high	low
Oranges	high	medium
Potatoes	medium	low
Tomatoes	high	high

I also have research indicating that organic produce has a higher vitamin content than non-organic counterparts. I think that could be a very valuable marketing point.

First, make sure you understand the question. You'll need to find items that are high in both vitamins A and C (*not* items high in one or the other or both).

Second, plan how to answer the question. You'll need to use *Vitamin Content* to find those items high in both vitamin A and C. Then calculate the revenue; you'll need to add up the percentages of sales for the relevant items and then multiply by the dollar figure given for total sales in the first paragraph of the *Sales* tab.

Finally, solve. Only tomatoes are high in *both* vitamins A and C. Tomatoes accounted for approximately 17% or 18% of total revenues (glance at those answers; you don't need to be very precise), so pull up the calculator and plug in this calculation: $0.17 \times 4441 = 754.97$.

The closest match in the answers is $775. The correct answer is (**A**).

If you feel very comfortable calculating by hand, the answers are far enough apart to estimate pretty roughly. For example, 10% of 4441 is about 444, so 20% is about 888. The answer has to be close to but less than 888; only answer (A) matches.

How to Get Better at MSR

The UPS process will help you both to answer the question and to review your work afterwards. If you answer a question incorrectly—or aren't fully confident about something you answered correctly—review each step of the process. Did you overlook, misunderstand, or fail to comprehend any information in the prompt? Did you answer the question that was asked? Was there a better way to approach the problem? Did you make any mistakes at the solution stage?

Test your skills with the below MSR problem.

Proposal | **Purpose** | **Budget**

The government of Storinia has proposed to conduct three particle physics experiments in Antarctica, as described below.

The *ultra-high-energy cosmic ray detector* (UHECR-D) will track a variety of subatomic particles with exceptionally high kinetic energy traveling from outer space by recording secondary showers of particles created by these UHECRs as they collide with the upper atmosphere of Earth.

The *polyethylene naphthalate neutrino observatory* (PEN-NO) will search for neutrinos, extremely light and fast subatomic particles that interact only weakly with normal matter. To prevent false-positive results from cosmic rays, PEN-NO will be buried deep below the ice.

The *magnetic monopole detector* (MaMoD) will attempt to verify the existence of magnetic monopoles, hypothetical subatomic particles that some physical theories postulate are left over from the creation of the universe.

Proposal | **Purpose** | **Budget**

The purpose of UHECR-D is to ascertain the identity, composition, and extraterrestrial origin of ultra-high-energy cosmic rays, which are much less prevalent and well-understood than lower-energy cosmic rays. PEN-NO will measure the mass and speed of neutrinos produced in particle accelerators and nuclear reactors, both to reduce uncertainty in the known mass of a neutrino and to contribute to the resolution of a recent challenge to Einstein's theory of relativity posed by the observation of neutrinos supposedly traveling slightly faster than light. PEN-NO will also measure the passage of solar and other neutrinos of astronomical origin. Finally, if MaMoD is successful in its search, it will provide experimental proof for Dirac's explanation of charge quantization and fix an asymmetry in Maxwell's equations of electromagnetism.

Proposal | **Purpose** | **Budget**

The government of Storinia projects that it will cost $42 million in total and take 2 years to construct UHECR-D, PEN-NO, and MaMoD. The government also projects that once construction is finished, the annual operating budget for each experiment will be $3.6 million for UHECR-D, $4.3 million for PEN-NO, and $2.7 million for MaMoD. All these figures are in real 2015 dollars (removing the effect of predicted inflation).

Example Questions

1. For each of the following statements, select *Yes* if the statement is supported by the evidence provided. Otherwise, select *No*.

Yes	No	
O	O	With a construction budget of $30 million, the Storinian government will be able to search for proof of an explanation of charge quantization and help resolve a controversy by measuring the speed of neutrinos produced in nuclear reactors.
O	O	In its Antarctic experiments, the Storinian government will attempt to ascertain the mass and speed of cosmic rays and confirm the composition of magnetic monopoles.
O	O	If the PEN-NO experiment operates on the surface of the ice in Antarctica, its findings will be considered more valid than those produced by the experiment as currently envisioned.

2. According to the information provided, the proposed measurement of which of the following kinds of particles is intended to improve the quality of estimation of the mass of these Particles?

   (A) Ultra-high-energy cosmic rays
   (B) Particles created by UHECRs above the earth
   (C) Neutrinos produced in nuclear reactors
   (D) Neutrinos that originate in the sun
   (E) Magnetic monopoles

3. For each of the following particle types, select *Can Conclude* if you can conclude from the information provided that the particles in question have a minimal effect on ordinary matter. Otherwise, select *Cannot Conclude*.

Can Conclude	Cannot Conclude	
O	O	Ultra-high-energy cosmic rays
O	O	Neutrinos produced in particle accelerators
O	O	Magnetic monopoles

How did it go? Before reading the following explanations (or even checking whether you got it right), you may want to review your work yourself. Then, you can use the below walkthrough to see whether you were able to catch any errors, traps, or other issues yourself.

Solutions

When you review your work, check whether your reasoning and understanding were accurate, not just whether you answered the question correctly.

Understand the prompt.

Proposal tab:

> *Storinia* is planning 3 experiments in Antarctica.
> Explains the 3 kinds of particles under investigation and in some cases how the experiments will work.

Purpose tab:

> Indicates the purpose of the 3 experiments.
> Explains how each experiment could be important to physics—the broader reason why they want to conduct the experiments.

Budget tab:

> Indicates the costs of the 3 experiments.
> Provides a link between costs and purposes (in the *Purpose* tab), so you can figure out how much it would cost to pursue various experimental goals.

Understand the question, plan, and solve.

1-a. No

Don't assume that the detectors cost an equal amount of money! Assign variables to the costs of the three experiments: $U + P + M = \$42$ million. You can assume that none of these experiments will cost $0 or negative (positive costs are a legitimate assumption). However, you can't conclude anything about $P + M$, other that $P + M$ is less than $42 million and greater than $0.

1-b. No

This statement is a classic case of mixing together unconnected topics from the passage. The passage indicates that the PEN-NO experiment will attempt to *measure the mass and speed of neutrinos*. The UHECR-D experiment says that it will try to *ascertain the identity, composition, and extraterrestrial origin of ultra-high-energy cosmic rays*.

Moreover, the MaMoD experiment will attempt to *verify the existence of magnetic monopoles*, not confirm their composition.

1-c. No

The *Proposal* tab tells you that *to prevent false-positive results from cosmic rays, PEN-NO will be buried deep below the ice*. This text implies that if PEN-NO is not buried in the ice, there could be *false-positive results from cosmic rays*. If that specific placement allows the experiment to achieve better results, then conducting this experiment at a different location will not result in more valid results.

2. (C)

The *Purpose* section, indicates that *PEN-NO will measure the mass and speed of neutrinos produced in particle accelerators and nuclear reactors, both to reduce uncertainty in the known mass of a neutrino …* . To reduce uncertainty in this known mass is to improve the quality of estimation.

None of the other particle measurements specifically mention mass. The passage says only that the *passage of solar neutrinos* will be measured; mass is not mentioned.

3-a. Cannot Conclude

The *Proposal* section indicates that ultra-high-energy cosmic rays create *secondary showers of particles … as they collide with the upper atmosphere of Earth.* So you cannot conclude that these UHECRs only have a minimal effect on ordinary matter.

3-b. Can Conclude

The *Proposal* section indicates that neutrinos are *extremely light and fast subatomic particles that interact only weakly with normal matter.* In the *Purpose* tab, a distinction is made between two sources of neutrinos. However, both kinds of neutrinos are neutrinos, so you can safely conclude that either kind has only a minimal effect on ordinary matter.

3-c. Cannot Conclude

The passage does not indicate what kind of effect these magnetic monopoles will have on ordinary matter. All you really know is that they are *hypothetical* and that if they are discovered, various theoretical implications will ensue.

That was a very challenging MSR question. If you struggled with it, notice a couple of things that might help you next time around.

First, while the tabs did have very detailed scientific information, you didn't have to become an expert in particle physics in order to answer all of the questions. The technical language was often just window dressing. For instance, in problem 1, the first statement mentions *charge quantization*, among other details, but you don't need to know anything about the details to know that you don't know how much each of the three experiments will cost separately. Likewise, you can get through the second and third statements of this problem without having to understand all of the details.

The third question could be pretty challenging but note that, in the end, the one that can be concluded says so in pretty straightforward language. The other two don't mention interactions with ordinary or normal matter. They could perhaps have done this using much more complicated language, but they didn't. The test writers just want to see whether you can read around the scary technical language and still process the high-level information.

In short, when you're done answering an MSR question (or any GMAT question!), your learning has just begun. Take the time to pick apart the prompt, the question, and your own reasoning in order to get better the next time you tackle a crazy science MSR question.

4

Next Steps

You're ready to start practicing! You have access to online Question Banks in your Student Center on the Manhattan Prep website. If you are enrolled in one of our classes or our guided self-study programs, then you will also have additional resources available; follow the instructions on your syllabus.

You can also find official IR questions from several sources, including GMAC's *Official Guide for GMAT Review* and the GMATPrep® software. The basic software comes with a number of free questions; you can also purchase additional questions.

Practice problems under timed conditions, one by one at first. Later, you may want to do a mixed set of four or five questions in a row. When taking practice tests, don't skip the IR section—if you do, then you may not be as mentally fatigued as usual when you get to the later sections, resulting in an artificially inflated score on Quant and Verbal.

4

Chapter *of* 5

Integrated Reasoning

Table Analysis

In This Chapter...

Chapter 5

Table Analysis

Table Analysis (Table) prompts, unsurprisingly, ask you to analyze tables of information.

The prompt will appear on the left side of the screen; the question will appear on the right side of the screen. Table prompts are always accompanied by one three-part opposite-answer question (e.g., true/false, yes/no).

You'll be able to sort the data by column, but if you're an advanced Excel user, you'll find the sorting very limited: the sorts will always be ascending, and you can perform only one sort at a time (no secondary sorts).

The table can be presented alone or with an associated blurb, which can range from a simple title to a full paragraph of information that you must understand in order to work with the table.

How to Tackle Tables

As discussed in Chapter 3, "Introduction to Integrated Reasoning," you'll use the UPS process to solve all IR problems, including Tables. UPS stands for understand the prompt, understand the question, plan, and solve. (If you skipped that chapter, you may want to go back andread the How to Tackle IR section.)

Table questions usually have a quantitative focus, often testing general statistics (mean, median, standard deviation, range, correlation, and so on) and Fractions, Decimals, & Percents (FDPs) (proportions, ratios, and so on).

Step 1: Understand the prompt.

Take a look at the following Table prompt:

> The table below displays data from the different divisions of Company X in 2011. Market shares are computed by dividing Company X's total sales (in dollars) for that division by the total sales (in dollars) made by all companies selling products in that category. Market shares are separately calculated for the world (global market share) and for the United States (U.S. market share). Ranks are calculated relative to all companies competing in a particular market.

Division	Global Market Share	Global Market Rank	U.S. Market Share	U.S. Market Rank
Agriculture & Food	8%	6	12%	4
Healthcare & Medical	12%	4	18%	2
Household Goods & Personal Care	5%	5	10%	4
Performance Plastics	30%	1	26%	1
Water & Process Solutions	19%	1	32%	1

If the table is presented alongside a title or informational text, begin by reading the blurb to set your context. If it explains specific parts of the table, examine the relevant parts as you read.

In this case, the blurb indicates that the table contains data about one specific company. Glance down and note that the first column shows the different divisions of this company. Next, the text explains how market share is calculated; glance down again to see that the table does indeed include columns for *Global* and *U.S. Market Share*. Finally, the text indicates that the ranking shows how this division ranks against all other companies in that market; again, the table shows two columns for this data, one *Global* and one for the *U.S.*

Finally, look over the full table to make sure you know the kind of data you have and how it is presented.

Step 2: Understand the question.

Here is the question:

Select *Yes* if the statement can be proven true for Company X in 2011 based on the information provided in the table. Otherwise, select *No*.

Yes	No	
O	O	There is a positive correlation between Global Market Share and U.S. Market Share.
O	O	Considering only Company X's divisions, the division with the median U.S. Market Rank is the same as the division with the median Global Market Rank.
O	O	The Performance Plastics division had greater market share in at least one other country than it had in the U.S.

This is an opposite-answer question. These questions will always contain two "opposite" answers, such as true/false, yes/no, or some other two-way split. Three statements will accompany the question; your task is to choose a single option for each statement. In order to earn credit for this question, you have to answer all three statements correctly.

The question asks whether you can prove each statement true based on the information provided. The *for Company X in 2011* language is typically just used to avoid having to repeat those details in each statement.

Next, scan through the three statements. On some problems, the statements are very similar and can be solved simultaneously or very similarly. On others, the statements are independent and must be solved separately.

In this case, the statements are fairly different, so work through them individually.

Yes	No	
O	O	There is a positive correlation between Global Market Share and U.S. Market Share.

What is positive correlation? If you've studied your statistics, you'll know that positive correlation occurs when two sets of numbers increase or decrease together.

Step 3: Plan your approach.

In order to figure this out, you're going to need to sort the table by either *Global Market Share* or *U.S. Market Share*—your choice (either will work).

Step 4: Solve the problem.

Here's the table sorted by *Global Market Share*:

Division	Global Market Share	Global Market Rank	U.S. Market Share	U.S. Market Rank
Household Goods & Personal Care	5%	5	10%	4
Agriculture & Food	8%	6	12%	4
Healthcare & Medical	12%	4	18%	2
Water & Process Solutions	19%	1	32%	1
Performance Plastics	30%	1	26%	1

As global market share increases, U.S. market share does generally increase, indicating a positive correlation. The correlation is not perfect: the second-to-last number in the *U.S. Market Share* column is larger than the last one. A small proportion of anomalies in the overall set is acceptable, though; as a general rule, the two numbers do increase together.

The answer to the first statement is *Yes*.

Evaluate the second and third statements in the same manner, repeating UPS steps two through four.

Yes	No	
○	○	Considering only Company X's divisions, the division with the median U.S. Market Rank is the same as the division with the median Global Market Rank.

The median is the number that falls in the middle when numbers are placed in increasing order. Sort by *U.S. Market Rank*:

Division	Global Market Share	Global Market Rank	U.S. Market Share	U.S. Market Rank
Performance Plastics	30%	1	26%	1
Water & Process Solutions	19%	1	32%	1
Healthcare & Medical	12%	4	18%	2
Agriculture & Food	8%	6	12%	4
Household Goods & Personal Care	5%	5	10%	4

The median is 2, which corresponds to Healthcare & Medical. Now, take a look at the *Global Market Rank* column. In a longer or more jumbled list, you might have to sort again by this column. In this case, though, the numbers are almost in order already. The median is 4, which also corresponds to Healthcare & Medical.

The answer to the second statement is *Yes*.

Yes	No	
○	○	The Performance Plastics division had greater market share in at least one other country than it had in the U.S.

In this case, you don't need to sort any columns; you can answer using just the Performance Plastics row:

Division	Global Market Share	Global Market Rank	U.S. Market Share	U.S. Market Rank
Performance Plastics	30%	1	26%	1

U.S. market share is 26% and global market share is 30%. You might have noticed that the other four categories all have larger U.S. shares than global shares, but the Plastics division is reversed.

MANHATTAN
PREP

The U.S. market is a subset of the global market, so U.S. sales will also contribute to the company's global share. Imagine that the global market consists only of the U.S. market; in other words, these kinds of plastics are sold only in the U.S. and nowhere else. In that case, the company's U.S. market share would equal the company's global market share.

Next, imagine that one other country also participates in this market, but that Company X does not sell in that country. In that case, the company's global market share would be lower than it's U.S. market share because there is a larger market, but this company doesn't actually capture any part of the non-U.S. portion.

If the company did sell in that other country but had lower market share than 26%, then the company's global share would drop below 26% as well.

In fact, only if the company sells *more* in some other country can its global market share actually be larger than its U.S. share. That's exactly the case here: Company X's global share, at 30%, is larger than its U.S. share, so it must have a larger share of the market in at least one other country.

The answer to the third statement is *Yes*.

The answers are as follows:

Yes	No	
⦿	◯	There is a positive correlation between Global Market Share and U.S. Market Share.
⦿	◯	Considering only Company X's divisions, the division with the median U.S. Market Rank is the same as the division with the median Global Market Rank.
⦿	◯	The Performance Plastics division had greater market share in at least one other country than it had in the U.S.

How to Get Better at Tables

The UPS process will help you to both answer the question and review your work afterwards. If you answer a question incorrectly—or aren't fully confident about something you answered correctly—review each step of the process. Did you overlook, misunderstand, or fail to comprehend any information in the prompt? Did you answer the question that was asked? Was there a better way to approach the problem? Did you make any mistakes at the solution stage?

Try this problem:

> The table summarizes total sales information for a large U.S. production company for the first six months of 2014. The table also provides percent of total sales for the company's only three divisions (Electronics, Housewares, and Automotive). The company acquired the automotive division in March of that year.

2014 Monthly Sales by Product Line

Month	Total ($, thousands)	% Electronics	% Housewares	% Automotive
January	3,890	47.09	52.91	0.00
February	4,204	49.75	50.25	0.00
March	6,561	34.19	33.00	32.81
April	6,982	36.44	34.03	29.53
May	6,613	37.97	33.34	28.69
June	7,028	34.58	34.00	31.42

For each of the following statements, select *Would Help Explain* if the statement would, if true, help explain some of the information in the table. Otherwise, select *Would Not Help Explain*.

Would Help Explain	Would Not Help Explain	
O	O	Consumer purchases of electronics typically drop just after the month of December, but they revive within two to three months.
O	O	Consumers tend to delay Electronics purchases when facing significant Automotive expenditures.
O	O	The Housewares division took a $1.1 million loss in March due to a product recall.

How did it go? Before reading the below explanations (or even checking whether you got it right), you may want to review your work yourself. Then, you can use the below walkthrough to see whether you were able to catch any errors, traps, or other issues yourself.

Step 1: Understand the prompt.

The blurb accompanying the prompt is fairly basic; it provides total and percent of sales numbers across six months. It also explains why the Automotive division seemingly had no sales in January and February.

The Total column shows a significant jump in March, corresponding with the acquisition of the new division. Other than that, sales are generally increasing, though May shows a drop. The Electronics and Housewares columns appear to drop in March, but this occurs because a third division is added; sales haven't necessarily dropped in the other two divisions.

Be especially careful with any questions that ask you to bridge the pre- and post-acquisition periods. You may have to do some calculations in order to be able to compare the numbers in a meaningful way.

Step 2: Understand the question.

The *if true* language signals that you need to accept each statement as true. If so, does that information help to explain some portion of the data that you see in the table?

Here's the first statement:

Would Help Explain	Would Not Help Explain	
O	O	Consumer purchases of electronics typically drop just after the month of December, but they revive within two to three months.

Step 3: Plan your approach.

If this is true, then January and possibly February Electronics revenues should be lower and then the numbers should increase in February or March. Check the data to see whether this trend exists.

Step 4: Solve the problem.

The Electronics percentage for February increased, as did total sales, so Electronics purchases did go up in that month. Did they go up in March as well?

In March, the Electronics percentage is now higher than the Housewares percentage. In addition, 34.19% of March sales is approximately $2.2 million, while 49.75% of February sales is approximately $2.1 million, so the trend continued in March (and April and May).

This statement does explain the data about the Electronics division. Select *Would Help Explain*.

Repeat steps two through four as you work through the second and third statements. Here's the second statement:

Would Help Explain	Would Not Help Explain	
O	O	Consumers tend to delay Electronics purchases when facing significant Automotive expenditures.

This statement essentially says that when auto expenditures increase, electronic expenditures should decrease. Sort the data by *% Automotive* and compare to the *% Electronics* column:

Month	Total ($, thousands)	% Electronics	% Housewares	% Automotive
January	3,890	47.09	52.91	0.00
February	4,204	49.75	50.25	0.00
May	6,613	37.97	33.34	28.69
April	6,982	36.44	34.03	29.53
June	7,028	34.58	34.00	31.42
March	6,561	34.19	33.00	32.81

Indeed, as the Automotive division's share of revenue increases, the Electronics division's share of revenue decreases. This also helps to explain the data in the table. Select *Would Help Explain*.

Here's the third statement:

Would Help Explain	Would Not Help Explain	
O	O	The Housewares division took a $1.1 million loss in March due to a product recall.

If there was a product recall, then perhaps that explains the revenue drop in March?

Be careful! It's not immediately apparent that revenue did drop. The Housewares *percentage* dropped, but the Automotive division was added that month. You'll have to crunch some numbers to tell.

Housewares accounted for approximately 50% of revenues in February, or about $2.1 million. The division accounted for 33% of revenues in March (pull out your calculator), or about $2.2 million. Housewares revenues went *up* a bit from February to March.

Perhaps the recall didn't affect other purchases. In any event, this statement does not explain the data in the table. Select *Would Not Help Explain*.

MANHATTAN
PREP

The answers are:

Would Help Explain	Would Not Help Explain	
◉	○	Consumer purchases of electronics typically drop just after the month of December, but they revive within two to three months.
◉	○	Consumers tend to delay Electronics purchases when facing significant Automotive expenditures.
○	◉	The Housewares division took a $1.1 million loss in March due to a product recall.

If you made a mistake at any step along the way, first try to isolate the error. If you fell into a trap because of the confusing data switch in March, when the Automotive division was added, you may have been able to anticipate such a trap by examining the data in a bit more detail before going to the question. The two 0.00% entries stand out, so try to understand what's going on before you go to the question.

Note that when a table adds a set of data part-way through, you can't compare the data sets as easily, particularly when the percentages have to add up to 100% (as in this case). Expect at least one of the statements to hinge around that change and be prepared to do a little number crunching.

Don't hesitate to pop up the on-screen calculator when you need it—just make sure that you know what you need to calculate before you start punching numbers. Also, you can estimate at times: 50.25% is close enough to 50% to estimate and you can find 50% without having to use the calculator.

Next Steps

You're ready to start practicing! You have access to online Question Banks in your Student Center on the Manhattan Prep website. If you are enrolled in one of our classes or our guided self-study programs, then you will also have additional resources available; follow the instructions on your syllabus.

You can also find official IR questions from several sources, including GMAC's *Official Guide for GMAT Review* and the GMATPrep® software. The basic software comes with a number of free questions; you can also purchase additional questions.

Practice problems under timed conditions, one by one at first. Later, you may want to do a mixed set of four or five questions in a row. When taking practice tests, don't skip the IR section—if you do, then you may not be as mentally fatigued as usual when you get to the later sections, resulting in an artificially inflated score on Quant and Verbal.

Chapter 6
of
Integrated Reasoning

Graphics Interpretation

In This Chapter...

<h1>Chapter 6</h1>

<h1>Graphics Interpretation</h1>

Graphics Interpretation (Graphs) prompts can be built on a wide variety of types of graphs, and you'll see many examples in this chapter.

Graph prompts consist of a graphic with some accompanying text and a two-part question, as shown below:

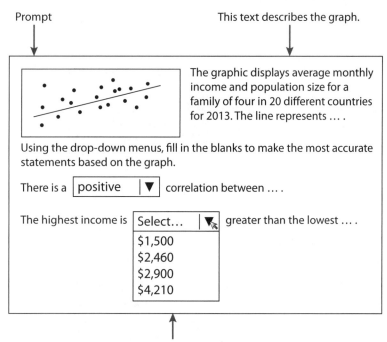

Most graphs are common types that you've seen before: bar charts, line graphs, and the like. Uncommon types could include Venn diagrams, timelines, even geometry diagrams. If you are given an uncommon graph, don't worry; you'll be given instructions as to what it is. Make sure to read any blurbs given with the graph.

The question appears below the graphic and consists of one or two sentences with two blanks. Your task is to fill in each blank with the best answer, chosen from drop-down menus containing three to six answer choices for each blank.

The two blanks may be related to each other, in which case you'll need to solve both simultaneously. The two blanks may also be completely separate from each other. In either case, you need to answer both correctly in order to earn credit on the problem.

How to Tackle Graphs

As discussed in Chapter 3, "Introduction to Integrated Reasoning," you'll use the UPS process to solve all IR problems, including Graphs. UPS stands for understand the prompt, understand the question, plan, and solve. (If you skipped that chapter, you may want to go back and read the How to Tackle IR section.)

Graph questions usually have a quantitative focus, often testing general statistics (e.g., mean or correlation) and Fractions, Decimals, & Percents (FDPs) (proportions, ratios, and so on).

Step 1: Understand the prompt.

Take a look at the below Graph prompt:

2013 Population 25 Years and Over

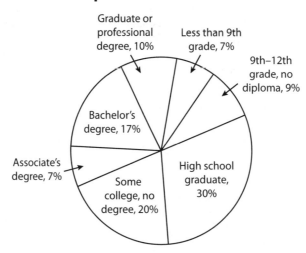

The percent of the population aged 25 Years and over that did NOT have a bachelor's, graduate, or professional degree is 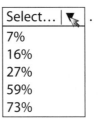 .

Select... |
7%
16%
27%
59%
73%

MANHATTAN
PREP

You will have to click on the Select button in order to see the multiple-choice options for that blank. Unlike the example on the previous page, an official question will have two blanks, each with its own set of options.

At a glance, you can see that this is a pie chart, one of the common types of graphs. First, read the title and any accompanying text in order to understand what the graph is all about. In this case, the title indicates that the chart provides information about a certain population in a certain year.

Next, dive into the graph itself. The wedges are labeled by type of schooling and show a percentage for each, but no real numbers. Since this is a pie chart, the percentages add up to 100%.

Step 2: Understand the question.

Before you read the sentence, click on the drop-down menu so that the multiple-choice options appear. Read the sentence with these options showing.

The question asks about certain categories of people: those with a bachelor's, graduate, or professional degree. Take careful note of that capitalized word NOT; the question is actually asking you to find the percentage of all others, not those three.

Step 3: Plan your approach.

Given that there are five categories in the "wanted" group and only two in the "not wanted" group, it will be far more efficient to add up the two "not wanted" categories and subtract from 100% in order to find the sum of the remaining five groups.

Step 4: Solve the problem.

Next, plug in the numbers and solve:

$$17\% + 10\% = 27\%$$
$$100\% - 27\% = 73\%$$

The correct answer is 73%.

Note that the answer choices are pretty spread out. You could also estimate on this one. The two "not wanted" categories add up to about 30%, so the rest have to be around 70%; the only close answer is 73%.

Types of Graphs

Some graphs will be very familiar to you; others will be unusual. You've probably seen a number of pie charts and bar graphs in your life, and you'll see these on Integrated Reasoning questions as well. Some IR graphics are frankly just weird. Some examples are shown below:

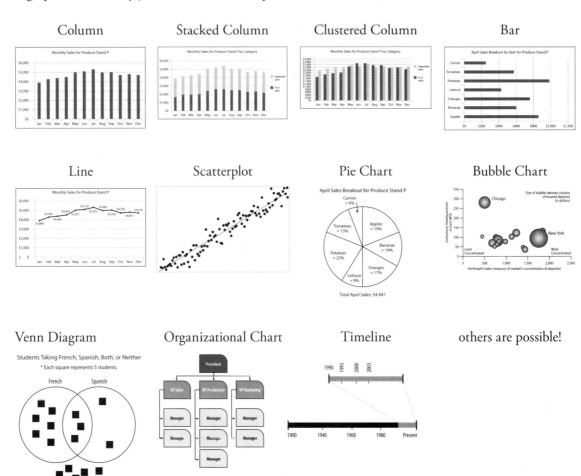

Don't let all these columns, lines, and bubbles scare you. These display formats are commonly used in business and academic settings today—and you've seen most, if not all, of these charts before. The GMAT will only rarely force you to figure out some really weird chart or graph. (*Chart* and *graph* are interchangeable words in this context.)

Column and Bar Charts

A column chart shows amounts as heights, highlighting changes in those heights as you read from left to right. Similarly, bar charts show amounts as lengths, highlighting differences in those lengths as you scan from top to bottom. For example:

Column

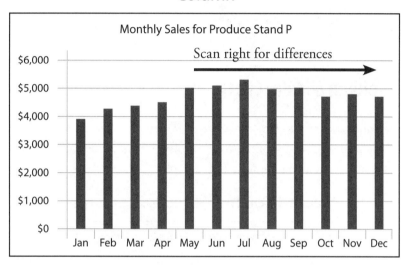

Bar

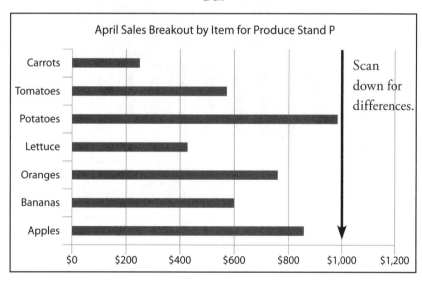

Column charts can be used to show trends over time, while bar charts are more frequently used for non-time comparisons (e.g., carrots vs. apples).

The hardest thing about a column or bar chart might just be reading a value from a column or bar that ends *between* gridlines. The GMAT will never make an exact value critical if you have to estimate, so just use your finger or your pen to make a straight line and take your best guess.

A question might ask you to calculate the percent increase or decrease from one time period to the next. Consider the monthly sales chart above, and answer the following:

What was the approximate percent increase in sales from April to May?

Estimate April sales to be $4,500 (the column ends about halfway between $4,000 and $5,000). May's column ends right on $5,000. Now use the percent change formula:

$$\frac{\text{May sales } - \text{April sales}}{\text{April sales}} \approx \frac{5,000 - 4,500}{4,500} = \frac{1}{9} \approx 11\%$$

Variations on Column and Bar Charts

If there is more than one series of numbers, the GMAT might use a stacked or clustered column chart. The stacked form emphasizes the sum of the two series of numbers, while the clustered form highlights which one is bigger at any point along the way. For example:

Stacked Column—*Emphasizes Sums*

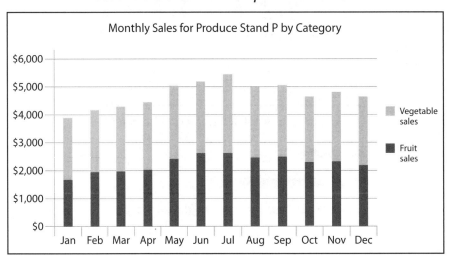

Clustered Column—*Emphasizes Differences*

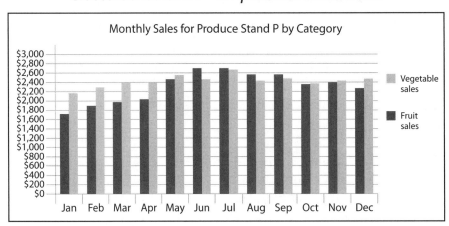

In the stacked column, it is hard to read off "Vegetable Sales" by itself—you have to subtract "Fruit Sales" from "Total Sales." Be ready to answer a question of this nature. Similarly, if you have a clustered form, you may have to compute the total on your own. The IR question writers will sometimes make you work against the grain.

Line Charts

Line charts are very similar to column charts. However, each number is shown as a floating dot rather than as a column, and the dots are connected by lines. The x-axis almost always represents time, since the lines imply connection. Although lines are continuous, do *not* assume that the data is itself continuous. If it is monthly data, it is monthly data—the line doesn't show you day-by-day. Multiple lines show multiple data series changing over time more clearly than clustered columns do. For example:

Line

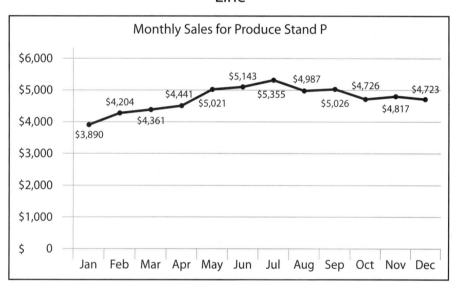

Line (with 2 data series)

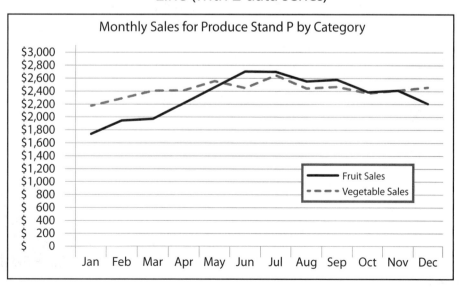

Scatterplots

A scatterplot is used to show the relationship between two columns of data in a table. Each point on the plot represents a single record (a single row). The overall pattern of the dots indicates how the two columns of numbers vary together, if at all. For example:

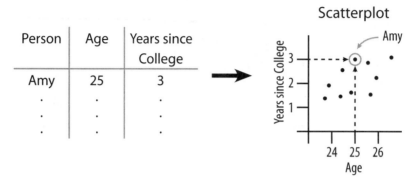

You might be asked whether the correlation between the two pieces of related data graphed is positive (slopes up from left to right) or negative (slopes down from left to right).

Pie Charts

A pie chart is used to show the relative sizes of "slices" as proportions of a whole. The size of the angle of the pie slice is proportional to that item's percent of the whole. Even if a pie chart shows amounts instead of percent, data is only shown in pies when percents are important to the story. The GMAT would *not* use a pie chart if the pieces of the pie don't sum up to a meaningful whole. Percents on various slices will always be the same percent "of" (the whole). For example:

Pie
April Sales Breakout for Produce Stand P

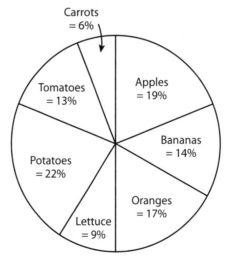

Total April Sales: $4,441

Since the total April sales figure is given, you can calculate the dollar sales of any item, or group of items, in the pie.

MANHATTAN
PREP

You might be asked to calculate absolute quantities from the percents given on the pie chart:

> What is the total dollar value of lettuce and tomato sales for Produce Stand P in April?

Lettuce and tomato sales are equal to 9% plus 13%, which sums to 22%. Remember, all these percents are of the same total ($4,441):

$$22\% \text{ of } \$4,441 = 0.22 \times \$4,441 = \$977.02$$

By the way, a pie chart can show only one series of data. If you see two pies, they represent two separate series of data.

Other Types of Charts

The list of possible graphics is not exhaustive; you may encounter a rare bird or beast in your IR journey. Don't panic. Read the title, read the labels, and try to figure out how the graph is laid out visually. If you're stuck, focus on just one small part, such as a single point. What does that point represent? What do you know about that point? Then work your way out from there.

Bubble Charts may look intimidating, but they are just scatterplots on steroids. Instead of two pieces of information about each point, you have *three*. In order to show that third dimension, all the little points are expanded to varying sizes—and those varying sizes give you a relative measure of that third dimension. For example:

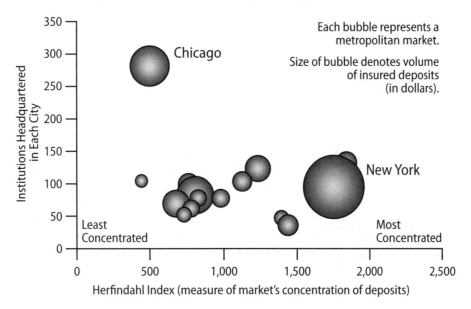

Bubble

Bank Deposit Concentration in Large Metropolitan Statistical Areas

Sources: Summary of Deposits, June 2002; FDIC's Research and Information System, June 30, 2003.
Note: Fifteen largest markets shown, based on number of institutions headquartered there.

6

Although this graph looks very strange at first, it is well labeled. Compare Chicago and New York. You can see that New York has far fewer bank headquarters (*y*-axis value) than Chicago does, and that less money (size of the bubble, or *z* value) is deposited among more banks in Chicago than in New York. Finally, Chicago deposits are less concentrated (*x*-axis value) than New York deposits are.

You may have run across Venn diagrams during your study for the Quant portion of the exam. Venn diagrams consist of two (or three) overlapping circles, showing how two (or three) groups overlap. For example:

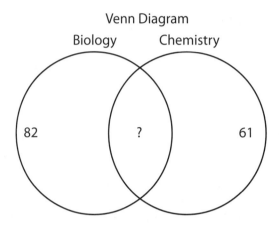

This Venn diagram indicates that there are 82 people in the biology-only group and 61 in the chemistry-only group. The diagram would be accompanied by a blurb providing additional information, possibly asking you to calculate the number of people in both groups (or in neither).

The organizational (org) chart and the expanded timeline shown below are good examples of unusual graphs that you can quickly decipher. Timelines don't have to run horizontally, by the way!

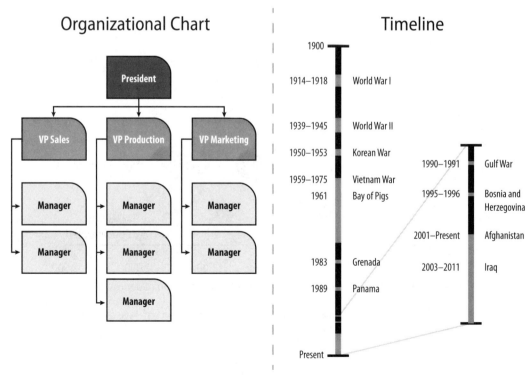

MANHATTAN
PREP

Typical org charts show hierarchical relationships within a business. Expanded timelines give you both a big picture of events in order and a "zoomed in" look at one part of the picture. Never forget that the scales in the different sections are different; be ready to make comparisons across those different scales.

How to Get Better at Graphs

The UPS process will help you to both answer the question and review your work afterwards. If you answer a question incorrectly—or aren't fully confident about something you answered correctly—review each step of the process. Did you overlook, misunderstand, or fail to comprehend any information in the prompt? Did you answer the question that was asked? Was there a better way to approach the problem? Did you make any mistakes at the solution stage?

Try another problem:

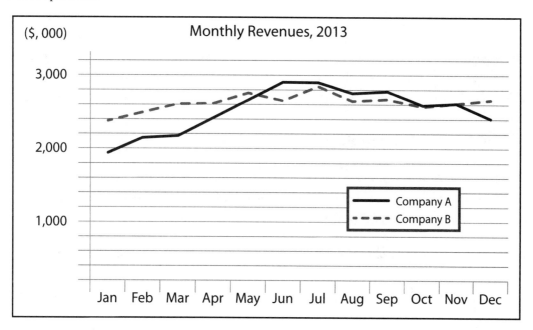

The chart shows 2013 monthly revenues reported by Company A and Company B, which compete in the cellphone market.

Based on the given information, use the drop-down menus to most accurately complete the following statement.

In 2013, Company A's annual revenues were [Select... | ▼] Company B's

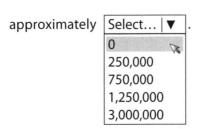

annual revenues and the positive difference between the two figures was

approximately [Select... | ▼] .

How did it go? Before reading the below explanation (or even checking whether you got it right), you may want to review your work yourself. Then, you can use the below walkthrough to see whether you were able to catch any errors, traps, or other issues yourself.

Step 1: Understand the prompt.

The line chart shows monthly revenues for two different companies. It's often very useful to count or calculate by increments on line or bar graphs, so figure out what each horizontal line represents and jot the figure down. In this case, each increment represents 200, or $200,000.

In some months, Company A earned higher revenues; in other months, Company B did.

Step 2: Understand the question.

On the real test, you will have to click on each blank in order to see the answer choices. Make sure you are viewing the answers as you read the statement.

The two questions ask for different things, of course, but the two blanks are related. When this is the case, think about how to save yourself some time and effort by solving the statements simultaneously.

Also, note that the answers for the second blank seem way too big. The *y*-axis is in thousands; these answers show the real number, not the abbreviated numbers shown on the graph. There is one bit of good news: these answers are very spread out, so you can estimate.

Step 3: Plan your approach.

The standard math way to solve would be to mark down every monthly figure and add them all up for both companies. That involves adding 24 figures, though—way too much work! There has to be an easier way.

There is! Count only the difference between the figures. Further, use the increments to make your calculations easier. Finally, don't worry about the *thousands* part of things for now; solve using the *y*-axis scale and add in three zeros later.

Step 4: Solve the problem.

Count by increments; later, you'll multiply by 200 to convert to the actual figure. In January, Company B is two increments above Company A. Because the first question asks whether A is larger, smaller, or equal to, track the difference in terms of Company A. After January, the differential is −2. The February differential is −1.5, so the total is now −3.5. Continue counting:

	Mar	Apr	May	Jun	Jul	Aug	Sep	Oct	Nov	Dec
Diff	−2	−1	−0.5	1.5	0	0.5	0.5	0	0	−1
Total	−5.5	−6.5	−7	−5.5	−5.5	−5	−4.5	−4.5	−4.5	−5.5

Company A finishes with −5.5 increments, or a total of (−5.5) times (200), which is equal to −1,100 below Company B. Add in three zeros, and Company A is $1,100,000 below Company B.

Thus, in 2013, Company A's annual revenues were ☐< Company B's annual revenues and the positive difference between the two figures was approximately 1,250,000 ▼ .

The increment method is a bit strange at first, but can ultimately make the calculations faster. Practice until you feel comfortable working with the numbers in this way.

You can also pull up the calculator and plug in each individual value to find the sums; only take the time to do this, though, if you have enough time. Don't sacrifice other questions later in the section as a result.

For the first blank, you can also eyeball the difference in area between the segments. For the first five months, Company A is significantly below, enough to create quite a large negative differential. Company B does lose some ground in the middle of the chart, but not enough to offset the initial differential, especially when Company B rebounds at the end.

You'll still have to dive into the numbers to answer the second question, though; you can't just eyeball that.

6

Next Steps

You're ready to start practicing! You have access to online Question Banks in your Student Center on the Manhattan Prep website. If you are enrolled in one of our classes or our guided self-study programs, then you will also have additional resources available; follow the instructions on your syllabus.

You can also find official IR questions from several sources, including GMAC's *Official Guide for GMAT Review* and the GMATPrep® software. The basic software comes with a number of free questions; you can also purchase additional questions.

Practice problems under timed conditions, one by one at first. Later, you may want to do a mixed set of four or five questions in a row. When taking practice tests, don't skip the IR section—if you do, then you may not be as mentally fatigued as usual when you get to the later sections, resulting in an artificially inflated score on Quant and Verbal.

6

Chapter 7 *of*

Integrated Reasoning

Two-Part Analysis

In This Chapter...

Chapter 7
Two-Part Analysis

Two-Part Analysis prompts closely resemble regular multiple-choice questions on the Quant and Verbal portions of the test. As the name implies, though, you'll be answering a two-part question.

The prompt will appear at the top of the screen with the multiple-choice answers in a table underneath, as shown below:

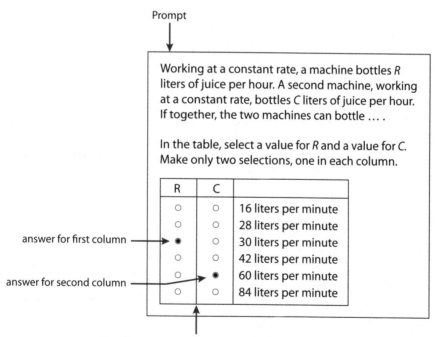

Two-Parts can be mostly quantitative in focus, mostly verbal, a mix of the two, or logic-based. You'll select from the same set of five or six answer choices to answer each of the two parts of the question. Depending upon the question asked, you may need to solve each part separately or you may have to solve the two simultaneously.

How to Tackle Two-Parts

Try this problem:

> Two water storage tanks, Tank A and Tank B, can each hold more than 20,000 liters of water. Currently, Tank A contains 5,000 liters of water, while Tank B contains 8,000 liters. Each tank is being filled at its own constant rate, such that in 15 hours, the two tanks will contain the same amount of water, though neither will be full.
>
> In the table below, identify a fill rate for Tank A and a fill rate for Tank B that together are consistent with the given information. Make only one selection in each column.

Tank A Fill Rate	Tank B Fill Rate	
○	○	30 liters/hr
○	○	90 liters/hr
○	○	150 liters/hr
○	○	220 liters/hr
○	○	290 liters/hr

As discussed in Chapter 3, "Introduction to Integrated Reasoning," you use the UPS process to solve all IR problems, including Two-Parts. UPS stands for understand the prompt, understand the question, plan, and solve. (If you skipped that chapter, you may want to go back and read the How to Tackle IR section.)

Steps 1 & 2: Understand the prompt and question.

Unless the question stem adds a lot of extra information, you can combine steps 1 and 2 for Two-Part problems.

Before you start to read a Two-Part prompt, glance at the answers. What form are they in? In this case, they're numbers. This quick glance will give you an early clue that you've got a Quant-based problem, and one that might be a rates problem, since the answers are in liters per hour.

Treat this like you would a standard Quant Word Problem and translate the information carefully on your scrap paper. Consider drawing a picture like the one below to keep the information straight:

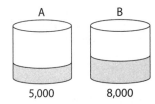

The two tanks are filling at different rates. In 15 hours, they'll have the same amount of water. What does that tell you about the rate for each tank?

Because Tank A has less water than Tank B to start, it must be filling at a faster rate. Keep that in mind or jot a note on your scrap paper; if your answers don't match that idea, then you'll know you made a mistake somewhere.

Step 3: Plan your approach.

This is a work problem, so you'll probably need the RTW formula: Rate × Time = Work.

How are you going to go from a starting point of 5,000 and 8,000 liters to an ending point of the same number of liters?

Use variables to set up a mathematical representation for the final number of liters for Tank A, in terms of Tank A's rate, and the final number of liters for Tank B, in terms of Tank B's rate. Then set those two numbers equal.

Step 4: Solve the problem.

Let's say that Tank A is filling at the rate of a liters per hour. Over 15 hours, it will add $15a$ liters. It started with 5,000 liters, so Tank A's final amount of water is equal to $5{,}000 + 15a$.

If Tank B is filling at the rate of b liters per hour, then it will wind up with $8{,}000 + 15b$ liters. Now set the equations equal to each other:

$$5{,}000 + 15a = 8{,}000 + 15b$$

But wait a second—that equation can't be solved for a and b individually. Now what?

Note that the question asks for fill rates that are *consistent* with the given information. That is, it doesn't just ask what the two rates *are*. This language is a big clue: the two rates are connected and there are multiple possible solutions, but there is a consistent relationship between the two rates. Your task is to figure out what that relationship is.

$5{,}000 + 15a = 8{,}000 + 15b$
$15a = 3{,}000 + 15b$ Subtract 5,000 from each side.
$15a - 15b = 3{,}000$ Subtract $15b$ from each side.

Remember that you already know Tank A's rate has to be higher than Tank B's, so $15a$ must be bigger than $15b$. As a result, you want to rearrange the equation to read $15a - 15b$, not the reverse.

Divide everything by 15:

$$a - b = 200$$

The two rates have to be 200 units apart. Look at the answers. The only two that work are 90 and 290, so fill in the circles:

Tank A Fill Rate	Tank B Fill Rate	
○	○	30 liters/hr
○	◉	90 liters/hr
○	○	150 liters/hr
○	○	220 liters/hr
◉	○	290 liters/hr

Double-check that you filled in the right columns with the appropriate numbers! Tank A has to have the higher rate.

How to Get Better at Two-Parts

The UPS process will help you to both answer the question and review your work afterwards. If you answer a question incorrectly—or aren't fully confident about something you answered correctly—review each step of the process. Did you overlook, misunderstand, or fail to comprehend any information in the prompt? Did you answer the question that was asked? Was there a better way to approach the problem? Did you make any mistakes at the solution stage?

Try this problem:

> Software Company M accused Company S of intellectual property theft, citing as evidence similar user interface designs for the company's new operating system products, both of which launched this year, and the fact that Company M's chief designer defected to Company S nine months ago. Company S countered that the product was 90% completed by the time the former chief designer joined Company S, and that the designer was not allowed to work on that product in order to avoid any potential conflicts of interest.
>
> Select the additional information that, if true, would provide the strongest evidence *For* Company S's claim that it did not illegally obtain information about Company M's products, and select the additional information that, if true, would provide the strongest evidence *Against* that claim.

For	Against	
○	○	A comparison with a third operating system company's user interface design shows overlap with Company M only in features that have been in industry-wide use for years.
○	○	Company S's former chief designer quit after a dispute over creative control.
○	○	Last year, another company released software that incorporates some of the same user interface designs at issue in the dispute.

MANHATTAN
PREP

○	○	Several key parts of the software code in Company S's product are nearly identical to code that Company M's former chief designer wrote for that company.
○	○	It is quite common for software companies to accuse other companies of intellectual property theft.

How did it go? Before reading the below explanations (or even checking whether you got it right), you may want to review your work yourself. Then, you can use the below walkthrough to see whether you were able to catch any errors, traps, or other issues yourself.

Step 1: Understand the prompt.

This Verbal Two-Part is pretty complex. It's also pretty similar to a Critical Reasoning (CR) problem, so tackle this in the same way that you tackle CR.

Read the argument and take some notes:

> M: S stole our design
>
> > 1. Similar design
> >
> > 2. M's designer → S
>
> S: 90% done; designer not allowed to work on it

Step 2: Understand the question.

The question does provide extra information, so read it carefully. The first part asks you to strengthen Company S's claim that it did *not* steal anything from Company M; in other words, the question is turning the argument around. The second part asks you to weaken that same claim.

Step 3: Plan your approach.

You can use the same solution standards for CR problems. A Strengthen answer makes the conclusion at least a little more likely to be valid, so the first column will validate (at least a little) the claim that Company S did *not* steal from Company M. Look through the answers now, concentrating just on this one.

Step 4: Solve the problem.

If you're very good at CR, you can try to find the strengthen and weaken answers at the same time. If, on the other hand, you have ever accidentally picked a strengthen answer when you were supposed to weaken, or vice versa, then concentrate on finding the first answer first (though you may sometimes be able to spot both answers on your first time through the answers).

As you read each answer, ask yourself whether it makes Company S's case any better:

7

(A) A third company's system doesn't overlap much with Company M's system. A *lack* of overlap doesn't strengthen Company S's case.

(B) Careful! Company S's designer quit—not Company M's designer, the one who moved over to Company S. The reason Company S's old designer quit has no bearing on what happened when Company M's designer joined.

(C) A third company released software *last* year that contains some of these same designs. The argument states that Company M released its own software *this* year, so this certainly bolsters Company S's claim that it did not steal anything from Company M (though maybe they both stole ideas from the third company!). Mark this one but check the final two answers.

(D) If some parts of the software code are identical to code written by Company M's former chief designer while working for that company, this definitely does not help Company S's claim that it didn't steal any ideas.

(E) This may be true, but it does not provide any evidence as to what happened in the specific case discussed in the argument.

Think back over your analysis. Answers (B) and (E) were irrelevant one way or the other, so they can't be the *Against* answer. If answer (C) is the *For* answer, then it can't also be the *Against* answer. Check (A) and (D):

(A) This choice does *not* actively weaken Company S's claim that it didn't do anything wrong.

(D) This choice does actively weaken Company S's claim. Identical pieces of code are a pretty big coincidence.

The answers are:

For	Against	
O	O	A comparison with a third operating system company's user interface design shows overlap with Company M only in features that have been in industry-wide use for years.
O	O	Company S's former chief designer quit after a dispute over creative control.
◉	O	Last year, another company released software that incorporates some of the same user interface designs at issue in the dispute.
O	◉	Several key parts of the software code in Company S's product are nearly identical to code that Company M's former chief designer wrote for that company.
O	O	It is quite common for software companies to accuse other companies of intellectual property theft.

Some Two-Part questions will ask you for two connected answers, as you saw in the Quant question earlier in the chapter. A verbal-based Two-Part might ask you to find a specific *cause-and-effect* sequence or a certain *characteristic* or *circumstance* that would lead to a specific *prediction*. In these cases, you will have to think about the two parts of the question simultaneously.

Others will ask you for two unconnected answers, as the last problem did. In these cases, you can sometimes save time by thinking about the two parts simultaneously, but if you ever make mistakes with this (for example, if you swapped the two answers on the last problem), then tackle the two questions separately in the future.

Try one more:

> A chemical plant operating continuously has two 12-hour shifts, a day shift and a night shift, during each of which as many as five chemicals can be produced. Equipment limitations and safety regulations impose constraints on the types of chemicals that can be produced during the same shift. No more than two oxidizers can be produced per shift; the same limit holds true for monomers. On either shift, the sum of fire protection standards for all chemicals should be no greater than 13 for health risk, 12 for flammability, and 9 for reactivity.

Four chemicals have already been chosen for each shift, as shown below:

Day Shift

Acrylonitrile	(health = 4, flammability = 3, reactivity = 2, oxidizer = no, monomer = yes)
Chloroprene	(health = 2, flammability = 3, reactivity = 0, oxidizer = no, monomer = yes)
Hydrogen peroxide	(health = 3, flammability = 0, reactivity = 2, oxidizer = yes, monomer = no)
Titanium dioxide	(health = 1, flammability = 0, reactivity = 0, oxidizer = no, monomer = no)

Night Shift

Ammonium nitrate	(health = 2, flammability = 0, reactivity = 3, oxidizer = yes, monomer = no)
Phosphine	(health = 4, flammability = 4, reactivity = 2, oxidizer = no, monomer = no)
Potassium perchlorate	(health = 1, flammability = 0, reactivity = 1, oxidizer = yes, monomer = no)
Propylene	(health = 1, flammability = 4, reactivity = 1, oxidizer = no, monomer = yes)

Select a chemical that could be added to either shift. Then select a chemical that could be added to neither shift. Make only two selections, one in each column.

Either shift	Neither shift	Chemical
O	O	Chlorine (health = 3, flammability = 0, reactivity = 0, oxidizer = yes, monomer = no)
O	O	Ethylene (health = 3, flammability = 4, reactivity = 2, oxidizer = no, monomer = yes)

○	○	Nickel carbonyl (health = 4, flammability = 3, reactivity = 3, oxidizer = no, monomer = no)
○	○	Phenol (health = 3, flammability = 2, reactivity = 0, oxidizer = no, monomer = no)
○	○	Sulfuric acid (health = 3, flammability = 0, reactivity = 2, oxidizer = yes, monomer = no)
○	○	Vinyl chloride (health = 2, flammability = 4, reactivity = 2, oxidizer = no, monomer = yes)

Step 1: Understand the prompt.

A logic problem! These are different than any other questions you'll see elsewhere on the GMAT. The chemical plant has two work shifts, day and night. At most five chemicals can be produced during either shift. Four of the five slots on each shift are already filled, so you're looking to fill the fifth slot.

Not just any chemical can fill the fifth slot, though. You are given several constraints:

- No more than 2 *oxidizers* (whatever they are) per shift.
- No more than 2 *monomers* (whatever they are) per shift.
- Health numbers add up to 13 or less.
- Flammability numbers add up to 12 or less.
- Reactivity numbers add up to 9 or less.

Step 2: Understand the question.

You have to identify a single chemical that would fit *either* shift (there's only one) and another chemical that would fit *neither* shift (again, there's only one). The characteristics of each chemical in the list of six to choose from will make all the difference, obviously.

Step 3: Plan your approach.

Since this problem is about following a chain of logic, go ahead and figure out what *must* and *must not* be true about the fifth chemical, by applying the given constraints to the four chemicals you already have. Do this for each shift. Then, armed with new and *simpler* constraints about the fifth possibility for each shift, go through the list of six chemicals and figure out whether the chemical in question could be on the shift.

Step 4: Solve the problem.

Day: You already have two monomers, the most you're allowed to have, so the last chemical can't be a monomer. That's one constraint. The health numbers add up to 10, and you can have 13 at most, so the biggest possible health number for the last chemical is 3. Flammability adds up to 6, and the cap is 12, so you can have any flammability (the maximum flammability is 4). Likewise, you can have any reactivity (the numbers only add to 4, and the cap is 9). Thus:

> Day constraints: Can't have health = 4. Can't be a monomer.

Night: You already have two oxidizers, the most allowed, so the last chemical can't be an oxidizer. You can have any health number (cap of 13 minus the sum of 8, so you have room for up to 5) or any flammability number (cap of 12 minus the sum of 8, so you have room for up to 4). However, the reactivity number cannot be 3 or 4, since the cap is 9 and the other numbers add to 7. Thus:

> Night constraints: Can't have reactivity = 3 or 4. Can't be an oxidizer.

Now consider the *Either* answer. A chemical that could go on *either* shift must be neither an oxidizer nor a monomer, so you can knock out four chemicals quickly, leaving nickel carbonyl and phenol.

Which of these two chemicals is more likely to work on either shift? Check the one with lower numbers first. Phenol's health number is low enough (3) to fit the day shift, and its reactivity number is low enough (2) to fit the night shift. Phenol is the "*Either*" answer.

Nickel carbonyl must not work for one of the shifts. Does it work for neither shift? Check it out. Its numbers are pretty high all around: 4, 3, and 3. The day shift rules out a health number of 4, while the night shift rules out a reactivity number of 3. So this chemical turns out to be the *Neither* answer.

Fill in the table:

Either shift	Neither shift	Chemical
○	○	Chlorine (health = 3, flammability = 0, reactivity = 0, oxidizer = yes, monomer = no)
○	○	Ethylene (health = 3, flammability = 4, reactivity = 2, oxidizer = no, monomer = yes)
○	●	Nickel carbonyl (health = 4, flammability = 3, reactivity = 3, oxidizer = no, monomer = no)
●	○	Phenol (health = 3, flammability = 2, reactivity = 0, oxidizer = no, monomer = no)
○	○	Sulfuric acid (health = 3, flammability = 0, reactivity = 2, oxidizer = yes, monomer = no)
○	○	Vinyl chloride (health = 2, flammability = 4, reactivity = 2, oxidizer = no, monomer = yes)

Most Two-Parts will be of the Quant or Verbal varieties and will resemble the questions in those sections of the test. You can use many of the same strategies you're learning for the Quant and Verbal sections, however, some Two-Parts will be logic-based problems like the one you just did, and as you saw, they require their own process.

As with all Two-Parts, the logic-based varieties will sometimes have answers that are connected, in which case you'll need to solve simultaneously, and will sometimes have answers that are independent, in which case you can choose whether to try to solve simultaneously. It may take a little longer to solve completely separately, but you'll also be less likely to make a mistake.

Next Steps

You're ready to start practicing! You have access to online Question Banks in your Student Center on the Manhattan Prep website. If you are enrolled in one of our classes or our guided self-study programs, then you will also have additional resources available; follow the instructions on your syllabus.

You can also find official IR questions from several sources, including GMAC's *Official Guide for GMAT Review* and the GMATPrep® software. The basic software comes with a number of free questions; you can also purchase additional questions.

Practice problems under timed conditions, one by one at first. Later, you may want to do a mixed set of four or five questions in a row. When taking practice tests, don't skip the IR section—if you do, then you may not be as mentally fatigued as usual when you get to the later sections, resulting in an artificially inflated score on Quant and Verbal.

Chapter 8
of
Integrated Reasoning

IR Strategies

In This Chapter...

Chapter 8

IR Strategies

This chapter summarizes what you learned in the previous chapters and provides some strategies for managing your time and effort in the overall section and on the entire test.

UPS is your go-to strategy for both doing Integrated Reasoning problems and reviewing and learning from them afterwards. This chapter will summarize how to use UPS with the four IR prompt types.

Timing and Guessing

As discussed in Chapter 3, plan to guess on some number of questions in the section:

If your goal score is...	# of Guesses	Per-Question Time
6+	2	3 minutes
5	3	3 minutes 20 seconds
4	4	3 minutes 45 seconds

Before test day, know what your strengths and weaknesses are, so that you can choose to guess on the worst questions for you.

Are you

- generally better at Quant or at Verbal?

- comfortable with tables and/or graphs? (Then Table and/or Graph prompts are for you.)

- good at piecing together information from different sources? (Then MSR is for you.)

- comfortable with standard Critical Reasoning (CR) and/or Quant multiple-choice? (Then Two-Part prompts are for you.)

As you make decisions about which problems to try and when to guess, keep in mind that the main event is still to come: your Quant and Verbal scores are more important than your IR score.

Avoid the temptation to go all out on IR. Don't let yourself stubbornly push forward on a very tough question because you feel like you "should" be able to answer it. Your mental energy is finite; make sure you save enough to perform at your best during the Quant and Verbal sections. Pace yourself in terms of time spent *and* mental energy spent.

Multi-Source Reasoning (MSR)

Key details:

    2 or 3 tabs

Typically 3 questions:

- 1 standard multiple-choice
- 2 opposite-answer questions

MSR prompts will contain two or three tabs of information and are typically accompanied by three separate questions. One of the questions is usually in standard multiple-choice format, while the other two are typically opposite-answer questions (e.g., true/false, yes/no). An opposite-answer consists of three separate statements, each one of which must be answered correctly in order to earn credit on that problem.

You'll need some additional time up front to get through all of the MSR text, but this time is effectively spread across the three questions you'll answer, so you'll be able to get through everything in a reasonable amount of time.

Step 1: Understand the prompt.

Glance at the tab titles for a hint of the topics covered. Use the titles to help you label your notes (a mini-map of the tabs).

Dive into the first tab. As you read, jot down information on your scrap paper to help you figure out where to go when you get to the questions.

As you work your way through the tabs, think about the *What* and the *So what*: what does the tab say and what are the implications of that information?

After you've looked at all of the tabs, take a moment to think about how they interconnect. Then start the first question.

8

Step 2: Understand the question.

MSRs come with two different kinds of questions: standard multiple-choice and opposite-answer.

Multiple-choice: Tackle these in the same way that you would tackle Reading Comprehension (RC) questions, starting with understanding what the question has asked you to do.

Opposite-answer: Glance at the three statements before you begin to see whether they are connected or unrelated. If connected, you can solve them simultaneously.

Next, read the question stem to see whether it just asks a question or whether it provides additional information that you'll need to respond to the statements. Jot down any additional information.

Finally, jump to the first statement.

Step 3: Plan your approach.

Which tabs are you likely to need in order to address this statement? What information do you need to find in those tabs?

On opposite-answer questions, if you can solve some or all of the statements simultaneously, figure out which pieces you can solve together and in what order you want to tackle them.

Step 4: Solve the problem.

Finally, do the work! On standard multiple-choice questions, look at the relevant information in the tabs, try to formulate your own answer to the question, then look through the answer choices for a match.

On opposite-answer questions, tackle the statements together when possible or separately, if needed.

Table Analysis

```
Key details:

     Table—will need to sort
     One opposite-answer question
```

Table prompts will, of course, contain a table, along with one opposite-answer question (e.g., true/false, yes/no). An opposite-answer question consists of three separate statements, each one of which must be answered correctly in order to earn credit on that problem.

The table may also be accompanied by a blurb: a separate paragraph of text that describes the information in the table and may even provide additional information you'll need to answer the question.

Step 1: Understand the prompt.

Start with the title and blurb (if present) to orient you to the information given in the table. Then, scan the column headers and rows of the table, thinking about the *What* and *So what*. What types of information do they contain? What connections (if any) exist between the columns?

Once you understand the basics, glance at the data in the table. Are there any surprising data points (e.g., example, some entries of 0 or some entries that are very different than the others)? Don't try to figure out why these entries are what they are; just notice them and keep them in mind for later.

Step 2: Understand the question.

You'll answer one opposite-answer question. Glance at the three statements before you begin to see whether they are connected or unrelated. If connected, you can solve them simultaneously.

Next, read the question stem to see whether it provides additional information that you'll need to respond to the statements. Jot down any additional information. Make sure you understand what the question is asking you to do; then, jump to the first statement.

Step 3: Plan your approach.

If you can solve some or all of the statements simultaneously, figure out which pieces you can solve together and in what order you want to tackle them.

For the first statement you tackle, how should you sort the table to make your job easier?

For quant-based questions, can you estimate to arrive at an answer or will you need to do an exact calculation?

Step 4: Solve the problem.

Dive in! Sort the table and examine the data. If you have to perform a calculation, make sure to do so on your scrap paper, not in your head.

If you get stuck, think about whether a different sort of the data might help to unstick you.

8

Graphics Interpretation

```
Key details:

    Graph or diagram of some sort
    One fill-in-the-blank question
```

Graphs may consist of a standard statistics graph, a chart, a timeline, or even a geometry diagram. Anything is possible, but if you're given something non-standard, you will also be given instructions as to how to read the graph.

The question will consist of one or two statements with a total of two blanks. You'll fill in these blanks with answers chosen from a drop-down list, one for each blank. You may be given anywhere from three to six multiple-choice options for each blank.

The graph may also be accompanied by a blurb—a title or a separate paragraph of text that describes the information in the graph—and may even provide additional information you'll need to answer the question.

Step 1: Understand the prompt.

Start with the title and blurb (if present) to orient you to the information given in the graph. Then, examine the graph, thinking about the *What* and *So what*. What types of information does it contain? What does each point, line, bar, or bubble represent?

If the graph type is completely unfamiliar to you, it's okay to take a little more time to orient yourself. If you're still lost, though, guess and move on.

Once you understand the basics, glance at the data in the graph. Are there any surprising data points (e.g., some entries that are very different than others)? Don't try to figure out why these entries are what they are; just notice them and keep them in mind for later.

Step 2: Understand the question.

You'll answer one fill-in-the-blank question. First, read the question stem to see whether it provides additional information that you'll need in order to answer the question; jot down that information.

Next, click on the first blank to show the possible answer choices and read through the first statement (or part of the statement). When appropriate, click on the second blank to see those options.

Do not read the statement without looking at the multiple choice options! The options will give you something to work towards, and they may completely change the way you plan for and solve the problem. For instance, if the answers are values that are spread apart, you'll know you can estimate. Alternatively, you may have been expecting specific values but the blank actually contains qualifiers such as *greater than* and *less than*. How you solve is quite different.

8

The two blanks may be related, in which case you may have to solve simultaneously, or the two blanks may be independent. Know the relationship between the blanks before you start to solve.

Step 3: Plan your approach.

Which parts of the graph do you need in order to tackle the first blank? You may need just one or two of the bars, bubble, or whatever data points you've been given.

Do you just need to find or identify something, or will you need to perform a calculation? Can you eyeball or estimate values or do you need to be more precise?

Step 4: Solve the problem.

Again, make sure that you are solving in a form that matches the drop-down answers given. Do any calculations on your scrap paper and don't hesitate to pop up the calculator when needed.

Wherever you can save time and effort by estimating, do so!

Two-Part Analysis

> Key details:
>
> Similar to Quant and Verbal problems
>
> Answer a two-part question, not just one
>
> May be Quant, Verbal, or logic

Two-Parts are typically more quant-focused, more verbal-focused, or more logic-based. Quant questions will look very much like standard Problem Solving questions and Verbal Two-Parts will typically resemble Critical Reasoning questions. The logic variety doesn't show up elsewhere on the GMAT.

You'll be asked to answer a two-part question but you'll actually choose from among the *same* five or six answers for each of the two parts. Sometimes, the two parts will be connected and you'll have to solve simultaneously; other times, they'll be independent and you'll solve separately.

Steps 1 & 2: Understand the prompt and the question.

Start by glancing at the answer choices (this is also useful on Problem Solving (PS) and Sentence Correction (SC) questions). Do you have numbers? Words? Sentences? That will give you a quick idea of whether you have a quant-focused question or whether it's verbal or logic.

Next, as with CR and RC problems, read the question stem. What is the question asking you to do?

Quant-based: Asks you to calculate something; contains, numbers, formulas, and so on; may ask you to calculate connected values (such as an *x* and *y* that simultaneously make an equation true).

Verbal-based: May ask you a CR-type question (strengthen, weaken, find an assumption) or may ask you a connected question (such as cause and effect).

Logic-based: Asks you to complete some kind of scenario; may contain tables of information or lists of rules to follow.

As always, jot down notes as you read so that you're prepared for steps 3 and 4. Check whether the two parts of the question are connected or independent.

Step 3: Plan your approach.

For quant-focused and verbal-focused problems, you can use the same strategies that you use in the Quant and Verbal sections of the exam. If you need to solve simultaneously, figure out how to set up that solution or reasoning method before you start to solve.

For logic-based problems, you may be able to use the constraints given in the prompt to narrow down the possibilities of whatever scenario you've been given. Do this narrowing *before* you dive into the solution process itself.

Step 4: Solve the problem.

Again, use your standard solving techniques for quant- and verbal-focused problems.

For logic problems, you'll often use process of elimination. Now that you've got the scenario set up on your paper, go through the answers to see what will (or won't) satisfy the desired conditions.

Next Steps

What are your IR strengths and weaknesses?

You may already have a good idea. If not, see how things go on your next practice computer-adaptive test (CAT). When you're done, analyze those problems and figure out which ones are the hardest ones for you. These will be your *Guess* questions in the future.

8

Already scoring at your desired level?

If you're already scoring at or above your desired level for IR, then you don't need to do much more. Do continue to complete the IR section on your practice CATs, both to keep your skills up and to ensure that you're not artificially inflating your Quant and Verbal scores.

Haven't gotten to your goal yet?

If you are scoring below your desired IR score, then you'll need to turn some of those weaknesses into strengths.

If you are enrolled in one of our classes or our guided self-study programs, then you have additional resources available in your Student Center; follow the instructions on your syllabus.

If not, then you can set up your own IR study plan. Review the strategies in this book for whatever areas are giving you trouble. Make yourself some flashcards to help remember key points.

Then, practice your skills on problems and analyze your work. Use the online Question Banks associated with this book or official IR questions, which you can find in GMAC's *Official Guide for GMAT Review* online Question Banks, IR Prep Tool, and GMATPrep® software. The basic software comes with a number of free questions; you can also purchase additional questions.

Practice problems under timed conditions, one by one at first. As you improve, start to do mixed sets of questions, perhaps one of each type. You'll still guess on some questions, though which ones may change as your skills change. Each week, think about how your abilities have changed and what implications that has for your *Guess* questions on the IR section.

When taking practice tests, don't skip the IR section, even if you know that you haven't yet studied enough. If you do skip the section, then you may not be as mentally fatigued as usual when you get to the later sections, resulting in an artificially inflated score on Quant and Verbal. This will also be the best chance for you to test your progress on IR.

Once you get your practice score into the range that you want to earn on the real test, you can scale down your IR practice and keep your skills up by doing and reviewing the IR section during practice CATs.

8

Appendix A

of

Integrated Reasoning

How to Write
Better Sentences

In This Chapter...

Structure Your Sentences—Then Flesh Them Out

Pay Attention to Grammar (to a Degree)

Choose Your Words—and Vary Them

Appendix A
How to Write Better Sentences

No matter how you feel about the essay, why not learn how to make your sentences better in general? For one thing, your efforts will pay off on the rest of the GMAT: the more you understand about sentence construction, the better you'll be able to read on test day. And every part of the GMAT demands that you read sentences quickly and effectively.

By the way, if you're a non-native-English speaker, GMAC says that "in considering the elements of standard written English, readers are trained to be sensitive and fair in evaluating the responses of examinees whose first language is not English." In other words, you'll get a little consideration. How much? Probably not tons. The good news is that if you've learned English as a second language, you're conscious of the grammatical issues that can empower you to write better sentences.

Structure Your Sentences—Then Flesh Them Out

A sentence should represent a thought. Thus, the core structure of the sentence should represent the skeleton of that thought, stripped of all flesh.

To analyze a sentence quickly, break it into **topic** and **comment**:

Topic: what you're talking about
Comment: what you're saying about the Topic

Take the first sentence in the 6.0 example essay in *The Official Guide for GMAT Review*. Strip that sentence down to its essentials to find the topic–comment structure:

The argument ...	omits concerns.
Topic	*Comment*
"What are you talking about?"	"What are you saying about that argument?"

At the simplest level, the topic is often the bare grammatical subject, while the comment is the simple predicate (that is, a verb and maybe an object):

The argument …	omits …	concerns.
Subject	*Verb*	*Object*
"What is doing the action?"	"What action?"	"To what?"

Good sentences have obvious—and intentional—core structures.

Now, how do you expand upon the core? How do you put flesh on the bones? You have many options.

1. Make compounds with *and, or,* and other connecting words.

You can make compounds of individual words, such as nouns and verbs:

> The argument omits or downplays concerns.
> The argument omits both concerns and criticisms.

You can also make compounds at the sentence level:

> The argument omits concerns, and it downplays criticisms.

Use this latter construction sparingly as a device to lengthen your sentences. Rely more on the next two tools.

2. Add modifiers to describe parts of the sentence.

As you probably know from your preparation for Sentence Correction (SC), the simplest modifiers are single words (adjectives, adverbs, and possessives):

> The *author's* argument *completely* omits *valid* concerns.

Modifiers answer questions about parts of the sentence: *Whose* argument? *What kinds* of concerns? *To what degree* does the argument omit concerns?

Here are examples of more complex modifiers:

> The argument *of the author* omits concerns *about implementation*.
> The argument *that the author makes* omits concerns *that must be addressed*.

You can embed modifiers within other modifiers. The full first sentence of the 6.0 essay is nothing but a single Subject–Verb–Object core with modifier attachments. Here is that sentence in all its poetic glory:

The argument that this warning system will virtually solve the problem of midair plane collisions omits some important concerns that must be addressed to substantiate the argument.

The core of the sentence contains only four words: The argument omits concerns. The remaining words are all modifiers that add extra information to the core.

Modifiers are a great way to lengthen and enrich sentences. To add modifiers, ask questions of the parts you already have in place:

Which argument?	that this warning system will virtually solve the problem of midair plane collisions
What kind of concerns?	some important concerns
What do we have to do about them?	(they) must be addressed
Why do they have to be addressed?	to substantiate the argument

3. Add sentence-level subordinate clauses.

Words such as *because*, *since*, *if*, and *although* indicate logical connections between your thoughts:

The argument omits concerns, *although it has merits*.

Try putting concessions first, so that you can pack a punch with your subsequent assertion—and then follow up with evidence:

Although the argument has merits, it omits concerns. For instance … .

You can also use a semicolon to join two sentences, adding a relational word such as *therefore* or *moreover*:

The argument omits concerns; *moreover, it downplays criticisms*.

As you use all these tools, experimenting with lengthening sentences, you might find yourself going too far. Don't add just to add; make every word count.

If you have a cumbersome sentence, first try breaking it into more than one sentence. If that doesn't work, move the heavy stuff to the end. Shift the grammatical core up front, so that a reader doesn't have to wade through a whole lot of modifiers to understand the gist of what the sentence is saying.

Pay Attention to Grammar (to a Degree)

You need to know grammatical rules for Sentence Correction; you might as well apply this knowledge to sentence *construction*, too. Yes, you can make occasional mistakes with grammar in your writing, as noted earlier. After all, the Analytical Writing Assessment (AWA) rewards volume. If you have a choice between writing a new sentence and polishing another sentence's grammar, you should generally write the new sentence!

All that said, the better your grammar, the clearer your thoughts. Pay attention to the following issues.

Parallelism: When you use parallel markers, make the parts logically and structurally parallel:

    X and Y   X, Y, and Z   both X and Y   X or Y   not only X but also Y

Pronouns: The Deadly Five pronouns—*it, its, they, them,* and *their*—can cause serious problems in writing. Try to ensure that these words have clear, meaningful antecedents—the nouns that they refer to. For example:

> *Sloppy:* If cars go too fast on the highway, it can cause crashes.

What does *it* refer to? The highway?

> *Better:* If cars go too fast on the highway, crashes can occur.
> Cars that go too fast on the highway can cause crashes.
> Highway speeding can cause crashes.

Modifiers: Put modifiers next to the thing you want to modify.

Your essay does not have to exhibit perfect grammar to get a great score, let alone a decent score. Even 6.0 essays can have minor grammatical flaws, as you'll see below.

By the way, feel free to use the passive voice. For one thing, it's grammatically correct. More importantly, the passive voice in English provides a useful way of flipping sentences around, so that you can control the topic–comment structure as you desire. Both of the below sentences are correct:

> Highway speeding can cause crashes.
> Crashes can be caused by highway speeding.

Choose Your Words—and Vary Them

Words are like notes on a piano. Play them and play around with them to appreciate their resonance. For the AWA essay, it's worth distinguishing two categories of words: *signal words* and *substance words*.

Signal words indicate relationships to previous text. Signals are super-handy as you *read* academic text (for instance, passages in Reading Comprehension). The same words are also super-handy as you *write* that kind of text. Don't be afraid of telling your readers exactly where they are and what's happening. Here are some good signal words to use in your writing:

Relationship	Signal
Focus attention	As for, Regarding, In reference to
Add to previous point	Furthermore, Moreover, In addition, As well as, Also, Likewise, Too
Provide contrast	On one hand/On the other hand, While, Rather, Instead, In contrast, Alternatively
Provide conceding contrast (author unwillingly agrees)	Granted, It is true that, Certainly, Admittedly, Despite, Although
Provide emphatic contrast (author asserts own position)	But, However, Even so, All the same, Still, That said, Nevertheless, Nonetheless, Yet, Otherwise, Despite *[concession]*, *[assertion]*
Dismiss previous point	In any event, In any case
Point out similarity	Likewise, In the same way
Structure the discussion	First, Second, etc., To begin with, Next, Finally, Again
Give example	For example, In particular, For instance
Generalize	In general, To a great extent, Broadly speaking
Sum up, perhaps with exception	In conclusion, In brief, Overall, Except for, Besides
Indicate logical result	Therefore, Thus, As a result, So, Accordingly, Hence
Indicate logical cause	Because, Since, As, Resulting from
Restate for clarity	In other words, That is, Namely, So to speak
Hedge or soften position	Apparently, At least, Can, Could, May, Might, Should, Possibly, Likely
Strengthen position	After all, Must, Have to, Always, Never, etc.
Introduce surprise	Actually, In fact, Indeed
Reveal author's attitude	Fortunately, Unfortunately, *other adverbs*, So-called

Substance words contain real content. Our main suggestion here is to have a mini-thesaurus up your sleeve for certain ideas that you are likely to express—and re-express—*no matter what particular essay you must write.* For instance, you will need to have more than one way of making this point: "The argument is flawed."

Simply memorizing a list of synonyms and spitting them back out will do you little good. The 2.0 (*Seriously Flawed*) essay published in the *Official Guide* is riddled with these terms, seemingly as a substitute for thought. But you don't want to spend a lot of time searching for another way to say that an argument is *flawed*. Use these lists to free your mind up to do real thinking:

Argument is good:	sound, persuasive, thorough, convincing, logical, compelling, credible, effective
perfect:	airtight, watertight
Argument is bad:	flawed (of course!), defective, imperfect, faulty, fallacious, unpersuasive, unconvincing, ineffective; it over-generalizes, makes an extreme claim, takes a logical leap, makes an unwarranted assumption, fails to justify X or prove Y or address Z
really bad:	unsound, illogical, specious, erroneous, invalid, unfounded, baseless
maliciously bad:	misleading, deceptive
Flaw:	defect, omission, fault, error, failing, imperfection; concern, issue, area, aspect, feature to be addressed, opportunity for improvement
Assess an argument:	judge, evaluate, critique, examine, scrutinize, weigh
Strengthen an argument:	support, bolster, substantiate, reinforce, improve, fortify, justify, address concerns, fix issues, reduce or eliminate defects; prove
Weaken an argument:	undermine, damage, harm, water down, impair, remove support for; disprove, destroy, demolish, annihilate, obliterate

Practice swapping words in your emails. Use Shift-F7 (PC) or the Dictionary (Mac) to call up a thesaurus and avail yourself of the *treasury* of English words (that's what *thesaurus* means). Don't go too wild—no word is precisely interchangeable with any other. If an entry in the thesaurus is an attractive but mysterious stranger, either ignore it or, if you're interested in learning it, pull up the dictionary and confirm the core meaning of the word. Then dig up examples of reputable use in print, so that you learn the word's strength, spin, and tonal qualities.

In your essay, avoid slang and jargon. You risk confusing or even offending your readers. You don't have to stick to highly formal registers of English; feel free to use contractions (such as *don't*) and short, concrete words (such as *stick to*). However, only write what's appropriate for an academic paper.

Appendix B *of*

Integrated Reasoning

Quantitative Topics

In This Chapter...

Decimals, Percents, & Ratios

Statistics

Appendix B
Quantitative Topics

Decimals, Percents, & Ratios

If you are not already very comfortable with solving percent and decimal problems, review core GMAT Quant materials, such as the Manhattan Prep *Fractions, Decimals, & Percents GMAT Strategy Guide*. This section describes only the new wrinkles that Integrated Reasoning (IR) adds to these sorts of problems.

Here are the key differences in how the GMAT sections treat these topics:

Integrated Reasoning	GMAT Quant
Decimals and percents are encountered more often than fractions. Ratios are also important. *Example:* Which of the following stocks has the highest price-to-earnings ratio?	Fractions are as common as the others. *Example:* $\dfrac{1}{3x} + \dfrac{3}{4 + \dfrac{2}{x}} = ?$
Percent problems draw on real data in graph, chart, and paragraph form. *Example:* Was the percent increase in imports from China to the U.S. greater than the percent increase in imports from Brazil to the U.S.?	Percent problems can be more abstract. *Example:* If x is $y\%$ of z, what is $y\%$ of x in terms of z?

For both sections, you need to know standard percent formulas, such as the percent change formula: $\dfrac{\text{Change}}{\text{Original}} = \%$ Change. Be ready to compute percent increases and decreases on the calculator. For instance, if you need to increase 107.5 by 17%, you will need to multiply 107.5 by 1.17; punch the following into your calculator:

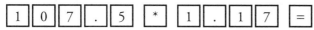

The result is 125.775.

Does 105.5 + 19% give you a larger result? Don't look for an estimation shortcut. Just punch it in and see. (It doesn't—the result is 125.545.)

Common Percent Question Traps

Here are four percent traps that you are likely to see on the IR section:

1. **Percents vs. Quantities.** Some numbers are percents. Others are quantities. Don't mistake one for the other, especially when numbers are embedded in text:

   > If a carrot has a higher percentage of vitamin A relative to its total vitamin composition than a mango does, does the carrot have more vitamin A than the mango does?

   It's impossible to tell because you don't know the total vitamin content of either the carrot or the mango. Perhaps carrots have a lot less vitamin content overall than mangos. A big fraction of a small whole could certainly be less (in grams, say) than a smaller fraction of a bigger whole.

2. **Percent of what.** Don't assume that all of the percents given are percents of the total. Some of the percents given may well be percents of something *other* than the grand total. If you miss that little detail, you will get the answer wrong:

   > If 60% of customers at the produce stand purchased fruit and 20% of fruit purchasers purchased bananas, what percent of customers did not purchase bananas?

   A casual reader might see "20% … purchased bananas" and decide that the answer must be 80%. However, the problem says that 20% *of fruit purchasers* purchased bananas. Fruit purchasers are a subset of the total—only 60%. The banana-buying percent of *all* customers is just $0.60 \times 0.20 = 0.12$, or 12%. The answer is 100% − 12%, which is equivalent to 88%, not 80%.

3. **Percent *of* vs. Percent *greater than*.** Try the following two questions:

   1. 10 is what percent of 8?
   2. 10 is what percent greater than 8?

   The first question asks for the percent *of.* The answer is 10/8, or 125%.

   The second question asks for a percent *change* or percent *comparison*. The answer is $\frac{10-8}{8}$, or 25%.

   The wording is very similar. Pay attention to the details!

4. **Percent decrease and then increase:**

> If the price of lettuce is decreased by 20% and then the decreased price is increased by 22%, is the resulting final price less than, equal to, or greater than the original price?

The resulting price is less than the original price, *not* equal to it or greater than it. In fact, if you decrease the price by 20%, you would have to increase the decreased price by 25% to get back to the original price.

Plug in a number to see for yourself. If you decrease $100 by 20%, you'll have $80.

You would have to increase $80 by $20 in order to get back to $100. Because $20 is 25% of $80, you would have to increase the price by 25%. Increasing $80 by 22% yields $97.60, which is less than $100.

Statistics

Statistics topics are important on Integrated Reasoning, since IR is all about analyzing real-world data.

Integrated Reasoning	GMAT Quant
Real-world statistical terms, including regression and correlation, are used to describe realistic data presented in tables and charts.	Statistics terms, such as mean and median, are used primarily to create tricky problems based on contrived data, such as sets of consecutive integers.
Example: The mean age of the participants in the marketing study is 24.	*Example:* How much greater than the mean is the median of the set of integers n, $n + 2$, $n + 4$, and $n + 6$?

When you have a lot of quantitative information, statistics can help boil it down to a few key numbers so that you can make good probabilistic predictions and better decisions.

This section covers essentially every statistics concept you need for IR. Most of the statistics questions on the IR section just require that you understand certain definitions.

Descriptive Statistics

Say there are 500 people in your business school class and you want to think about the *number of years* each of you spent working between college graduation and business school.

To make things simple, you'll probably round to the nearest whole number (instead of having data like 5.25 years, 7.8 years, etc.). Whole numbers are *discrete* (or able to be separated and counted), so with this information, you can make a *histogram* to display the count in each category.

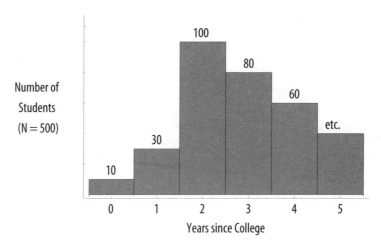

These three terms are very commonly tested on both IR and Quant:

1. Average (arithmetic mean)
2. Median
3. Mode

The arithmetic mean is the most important. You may already know the formula from the GMAT Quant section:

$$\text{Mean} = \frac{\text{Sum of all terms}}{\text{Number of terms}}$$

Add up everyone's "years since college" and divide that total by 500, the number of people in your class:

$$\text{Mean Years} = \frac{\text{Total years}}{\text{Number of students}}$$

$$3.36 = \frac{1,680}{500}$$

The **median** is the middle number, or the 50th percentile: half of the people have more years since college (or the same number), and half have fewer years (or the same number). If you have an odd number of terms, say {1, 2, 3, 4, 5}, then the median is the middle number (in this case, 3). If you have an even number of terms, say {1, 2, 3, 4), then the median is the average of the two middle terms (in this case, 2.5). The median of the Years since College distribution is 4 years because the 250th and 251st students are both 4 years out of college.

The **mode** is the observation that shows up the most often, corresponding to the highest frequency on the histogram. If none of the years to the right of 4 have more than 100 people, then the histogram peaks at this entry and the mode is 2 years.

The Spread

Mean, median, and mode are all *central* measures—they answer the question, "Where's the center of all the data?" But often, you need to know how spread out the data is.

The crudest measure of spread is **range**, which is just the largest value minus the smallest value. While range is easy to calculate, it's susceptible to **outliers**—oddball observations that, rightly or wrongly, lie far away from most of the others. For example, if one person in your program is in her 70s and has been out of school for 50 years, then your range of Years Since College would be huge because of that one outlier.

A better measure of spread is **standard deviation**. You will never have to calculate standard deviation on the GMAT because it is such a pain to do so without Excel or other software.

Roughly, standard deviation indicates how far, on average, each data point is from the mean. That's not the precise mathematical definition, but it's close enough for the GMAT.

For example, if your data points are {3, 3, 3, 3, 3}, then the standard deviation is 0, because every data point is 0 units away from the average of the set. If your data points are {1, 2, 3, 4, 5}, then your standard deviation is something larger than 0 (remember, you won't have to calculate it), because only one of the data points equals the average; the other four are more spread out. For example:

> Which data set has the higher standard deviation: {1, 2, 3, 4, 5} or {10, 20, 30, 40, 50}?

In the first data set, the numbers are very close to the mean of 3. In the second, the numbers are much farther away, on average, from the mean of 30. The second set has the higher standard deviation.

Standard deviation is incredibly important in finance, operations, and other subjects. For now, focus on an intuitive understanding. For instance, if you add outliers, the standard deviation increases. If you remove outliers, it decreases. If you just shift every number up by 1, the standard deviation stays the same.

Correlation

Up to now, everything has had to do with one variable—one measurement:

Student	Years since College
You	4
Anika Atwater	2
Bao Yang	6
...	...

One variable for each observation.

What if you get *two* pieces of data about each person? Now you can look at more interesting patterns:

Student	Years since College	Height
You	4	5 feet 7 inches
Anika Atwater	2	5 feet 10 inches
Bao Yang	6	5 feet 2 inches
...	...	...

To find a pattern, put all of these observations on a scatterplot:

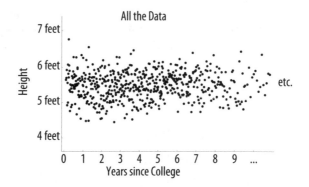

The "shotgun blast" shows that two variables, Years since College and Height, are basically **uncorrelated**. Numbers are correlated when they increase together or decrease together; in this case, there is **no correlation** because no such pattern exists.

In contrast, if you plot Years since College versus Age, you'll get a pattern. Typically, older people have been out of college longer:

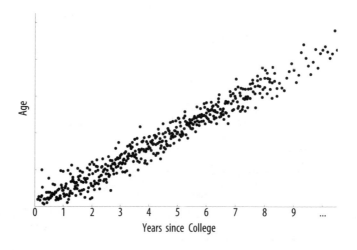

Most people are either high on both scales or low on both scales. This means that Years since College and Age are highly **correlated**. There is a **positive relationship** between the two variables.

If the data is presented to you in a table, you'll have to sort by one of the two parameters and then compare the two columns. If the numbers mostly increase (or decrease) together, then there is a positive correlation. If one increases while the other decreases, the two have a negative correlation. If no such pattern exists, the two metrics have no correlation. To summarize:

Correlation	Pattern	Example
Positive	Points cluster around a line of positive slope	
None	No pattern (shotgun blast) *or* a non-linear pattern	
Negative	Points cluster around a line of negative slope	

Regression

If you're asked to do a linear regression, you have to find the **best-fit line** through a scatterplot. With such a line, you can describe the relationship between x and y more precisely and even predict values of y from values of x:

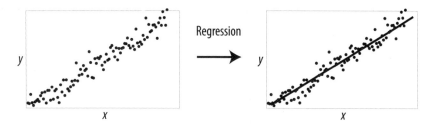

The best-fit regression line minimizes the distance, in some sense, between the points and the line. You can see this intuitively:

The GMAT will never ask you to compute a linear regression, but a graphical Integrated Reasoning question might ask about the slope of a regression line:

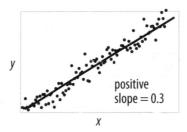

If *x* increases by 1, *y* goes up
by 0.3 on average.

If the two variables are positively correlated, then the regression line will have positive slope, demonstrating a positive relationship. Likewise, a negative correlation will have a negative slope of regression line and a negative relationship.

Remember that to find a line is to find its equation. The general equation of a line is $y = mx + b$. The letter *m* represents the **slope** of the line, while *b* represents the **y-intercept**, where the line crosses the y-axis:

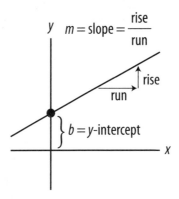

A line with the equation $y = 3x - 2$ intercepts the y-axis at $(0, -2)$. On this line, if *x* increases by 1, *y* increases by 3:

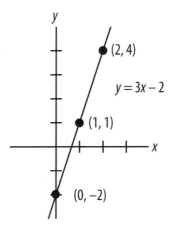

Finding the line means finding the values for the slope *m* and the y-intercept *b*.

GO BEYOND BOOKS.
TRY A FREE CLASS NOW.

IN-PERSON COURSE

Find a GMAT course near you and attend the first session free, no strings attached. You'll meet your instructor, learn how the GMAT is scored, review strategies for Data Sufficiency, dive into Sentence Correction, and gain insights into a wide array of GMAT principles and strategies.

**Find your city at
manhattanprep.com/gmat/classes**

ONLINE COURSE

Enjoy the flexibility of prepping from home or the office with our online course. Your instructor will cover all the same content and strategies as an in-person course, while giving you the freedom to prep where you want. Attend the first session free to check out our cutting-edge online classroom.

**See the full schedule at
manhattanprep.com/gmat/classes**

GMAT® INTERACT™

GMAT Interact is a comprehensive self-study program that is fun, intuitive, and driven by you. Each interactive video lesson is taught by an expert instructor and can be accessed on your computer or mobile device. Lessons are personalized for you based on the choices you make.

**Try 5 full lessons for free at
manhattanprep.com/gmat/interact**

Not sure which is right for you? Try all three!
Or give us a call and we'll help you figure out
which program fits you best.

Toll-Free U.S. Number (800) 576-4628 | **International** 001 (212) 721-7400 | **Email** gmat@manhattanprep.com

PREP MADE PERSONAL

Whether you want quick coaching
in a particular GMAT subject area
or a comprehensive study plan developed
around your goals, we've got you covered.
Our expert, 99th percentile GMAT tutors
can help you hit your top score.

CHECK OUT THESE REVIEWS FROM MANHATTAN PREP TUTORING STUDENTS.

CALL OR EMAIL US AT **800-576-4628** OR **GMAT@MANHATTANPREP.COM**
FOR INFORMATION ON RATES AND TO GET PAIRED WITH YOUR GMAT TUTOR.